MORE COUNTRY WALKS NEAR BOSTON

by
WILLIAM G. SCHELLER

Published by
THE APPALACHIAN MOUNTAIN CLUB
BOSTON, MASSACHUSETTS
1984

This book is for Mike Hoel and Bob Murphy, who know a good deal more than I do about many of these places, and are always willing to share that knowledge.

MORE COUNTRY WALKS NEAR BOSTON

Copyright © 1984 by William G. Scheller

All rights reserved.

Printed in the United States of America.

No part of this book may be used or reproduced in any manner whatsoever without the written permission of the publisher except in the case of brief quotations embodied in critical articles or reviews. If you find any errors in the texts or maps, or can suggest improvements, you are urged to send a letter to the Appalachian Mountain Club, attention Country Walks, 5 Joy Street, Boston, Massachusetts 02108. Due to changes in conditions, use of the information in this book is at the sole risk of the user.

FIRST EDITION

Editorial supervision by Sally Greene Carrel
Cover design by Hannus Design Associates
Photographs by Paul Mozell
Maps by David Cooper
Composition by Gayle Morrison and Anne Tuttle
Production by Michael Cirone and Nancy H. Maynes

ISBN 0-910146-51-9

10   9   8   7   6   5   4   87   88

CONTENTS

	Introduction	1
1	**Ipswich River Wildlife Sanctuary**	4

Walking and ski touring — ten miles of trails thread through a 2,000-acre wildlife sanctuary offering upland and freshwater marsh environments, non-native botanical species, an unusual man-made rock formation, and fine birding and canoeing.

2   Belle Isle Marsh 14

Walking — a living salt marsh, and one of the area's best birding spots, within the metropolitan confines of Boston, Winthrop, and Revere. A short walk traverses several plant communities, which illustrate the continued viability of this fertile and incongruous environment.

3   Brook Farm 24

Walking — a 2-mile round trip into the hills above the Charles River in West Roxbury, where George Ripley and his associates conducted a famous nineteenth-century experiment in communal living.

4   Lynn Woods 34

Walking and ski touring — a circuit of approximately 5 miles through the largest of all the Boston area's city parks, with stops along the way at a pirate's cave and two prominent vantage points.

5 Moose Hill Wildlife Sanctuary   44
Walking and ski touring — several miles of trails crisscross a small but ecologically varied Massachusetts Audubon Sanctuary in suburban Canton. Nearby is an interesting museum devoted entirely to whaling.

6 Lovells and Gallups Islands   52
Walking — two of Boston Harbor's smaller islands, now a part of a state park, offer camping, walks through woods and meadows, and a look at military ruins, all within a short boat trip and "water taxi" ride from downtown.

7 Peddocks, Bumpkin, and Grape Islands   60
Walking and (on Peddocks) ski touring — three more of the harbor islands, including the largest, a place of abandoned barracks dating from the era of the Spanish–American War, forested drumlins, salt marshes, and meandering pathways.

8 Ravenswood Park   70
Walking and ski touring — a rocky, hilly, heavily wooded 500-acre preserve at Gloucester's western threshhold, laced with miles of trails and eighteenth-century dirt roads. A short side trip takes you to the famous Hammond Castle Museum.

9 Ward Reservation   78
Walking and ski touring — a 3-mile ramble through a Trustees of Reservations property that contains both the highest point of Essex County and one of its fascinating low points, a black spruce bog.

10 Lowell   86
A city walk that leads both to the origins of large-scale industrialism in America, and to the earliest social and visual influences on an important modern writer. A national park visitors' center helps provide orientation.

11 Broadmoor Wildlife Sanctuary   98
Walking and ski touring — 9 miles of trails lead through historic grown-over farmland on the banks of the Charles River, and past the site of one of the area's early lumber and grain milling ventures.

12 Plum Island   106
Walking — one of the largest and best-preserved barrier beaches on the North Atlantic coast. Enjoy walks through or along primary and secondary dunes, salt and freshwater marshes, and scrub forest; also some of the finest coastal birding in the country. Nearby is Old Town Hill, where a short walk pays off in splendid views.

13 Hog Island   118
A combination canoe trip and walk, with the destination the least known, least accessible, and perhaps most beautiful part of the vast Crane Reservation in Ipswich and Essex. Visit a colonial homestead and walk to the top of a reforested drumlin for commanding views of the salt marshes, estuaries, and barrier beaches north of Cape Ann.

14 Winnekenni Park   128
Walking and ski touring — a visit to the land John Greenleaf Whittier loved, with a 3-mile lakeside

trail and other paths within a Haverhill city park that contains a restored stone "castle." Nearby are Whittier's Haverhill birthplace and, in Amesbury, his lifelong home.

15 Middleton Woodlots   136

Walking and ski touring — the Prichard and Captain Bill Woodlots, components of Essex County Greenbelt's system of preserved open spaces, offer access to Boxford State Forest from the south. A developing network of trails leads through one-time farmland now grown over with mixed hardwood and coniferous forest.

16 Ipswich to Newburyport:
The B&M Eastern Division   144

Walking or ski touring — follow the tracks for 11 miles from one old North Shore town to another, along the way enjoying seldom-seen perspectives of Essex woods and marshes and making some observations about the construction and maintenance of this now nearly abandoned rail route. If you wish, spend the night in a Newburyport inn and return the following day.

17 Whitney and Thayer Woods   154

Walking and ski touring — a circuit of approximately 2.5 miles, one of many that are possible within this Trustees of Reservations preserve of nearly eight hundred acres in Cohasset and Hingham. The woods cover a rocky, gently ascending terrain once farmed by South Shore yeomen and since reverted to forest.

18 Dogtown 160
Walking and ski touring — follow prerevolutionary pathways for 4 miles through a strange and desolate section of Gloucester and Rockport and past the ancient cellar holes that are the lone reminders of a vanished settlement.

Bibliography 170

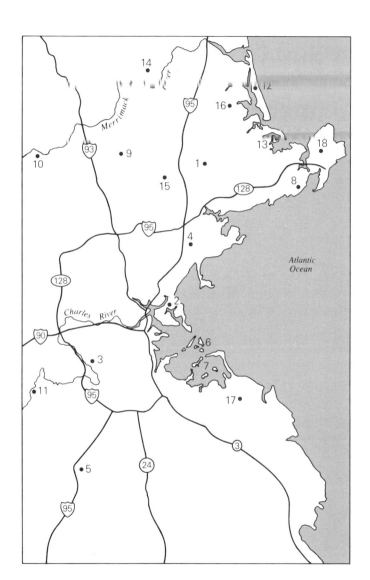

INTRODUCTION

Boston's legacy of land preservation is wise, foresighted, and nearly unique. Massachusetts learned its lessons early, and it learned them well. We have, of course, our share of Route Ones and Route Nines, with their orange dinosaurs and ten-acre steakhouses and gargantuan shopping malls. We have our 1950s subdivisions, clustered like grapes along the interstate highways. But we also have a remarkable amount of land that is safe from development, land banked like old China Trade fortunes against a time — today — when we knew we would need it for breathing room.

The continued accessibility of these places, like this book about some of the best of them, would have been impossible if it were not for the work done years ago by private and public organizations such as the Massachusetts Audubon Society, Essex County Greenbelt, the Trustees of Reservations, and the Metropolitan District Commission — the last two of which were the direct result of activism on the part of Appalachian Mountain Club members near the close of the last century. Not all of the places described here are the provinces of these groups, but even the ones which are not are open to us today because of the same practical intelligence and civic spirit which attended their formation. Anyone who cares about the outdoors and about the compatible goals of enhanced conservation and recreation has a lot to be grateful for in this part of the world, along with a responsibility to keep the tradition alive. This work isn't over yet.

MORE COUNTRY WALKS

Like the other books in this series, *More Country Walks Near Boston* is intended as part trail guide, part travelogue and part history. Some places lend themselves easily to specific directions; others invite do-it-yourself rambling. Many of the distances which can be covered in these walks are variable, and often the same area can offer a two-mile stroll or a ten-mile hike. Decide in advance how long you plan to be on the trail, so that you can work out transportation arrangements as well as lunch and clothing requirements. Most people walk at a pace of between two and three miles an hour; since the trips in this book are intended for recreation rather than rigor, the slower rate will more likely apply. Remember that snowshoeing or walking in snow or sand can take up to twice as long as a walk of the same length on hard ground. Conversely, cross-country skiers can often put distances behind them much more quickly than pedestrians.

Check weather forecasts before you leave for a walk, and dress appropriately. Take along a sweater or light jacket in the fall or spring, and wear sturdy, comfortable shoes or boots regardless of the season.

Always keep to established trails. At first, this admonition may seem to apply only to the pristine backwoods, but a minute's reflection should serve to convince walkers that open lands near large cities are every bit as fragile as the wilderness, and sometimes more so. Heavy use of these places can only be sustained if everyone treats them gently and stays on trail.

Public transportation information is given for some but not all of these destinations. Always plan ahead for your connections; nothing is more demoralizing after a day on the trail than finding that the last bus or train has left. Your main sources of public transit information will be the Massachusetts Bay Transit Authority (722-3200; 722-5000 nights and weekends), and the Boston and Maine Railroad (227-5070).

As always, the research of a book like this requires the assistance of a great many people. In addition to the two gentlemen mentioned in the dedication, I would like to thank Ralph Scott, Eugene Dooley, John Moberger, Mike Shannon, Catuhy Abbott, John W. Kimball, Bob Murray, Maude Salinger, Jim MacDougall, Liz Bell, George Anderson, Fran Belcher, Nathan Bates, Noel Ripley, Michael Westgate, and Barbara Gard, an active member of the Friends of Belle Isle Marsh. Barbara researched much of the ownership, social history, and natural history of Belle Isle, and most of the information presented in chapter two of this book was gleaned from her Master's thesis "Belle Isle: A Salt Marsh in a City," submitted in 1984 towards a degree in Urban and Environmental Policy from Tufts University.

W.S.

1

IPSWICH RIVER WILDLIFE SANCTUARY

Walking and ski touring — ten miles of trails thread through a 2,000-acre wildlife sanctuary offering upland and freshwater marsh environments, nonnative botanical species, an unusual man-made rock formation, and fine birding and canoeing opportunities.

TOPSFIELD'S IPSWICH RIVER Wildlife Sanctuary is, at 2,500 acres, the largest of the preserves owned and maintained by the Massachusetts Audubon Society. Its size, though, is deceiving: nearly three-quarters of the sanctuary is wetlands. This makes much of it only marginally accessible to the 75,000 visitors who come here every year; at this place, heavy use and a remarkably pristine environment manage to coexist.

If you approach the Ipswich River Sanctuary the way most people do, along the narrow road that leads from Perkins Row to the parking area and administration buildings, the topographical feature which will make the strongest initial impression will no doubt be Bradstreet Hill, upon which the buildings stand. Bradstreet Hill is a drumlin. Drumlins are smoothly rounded deposits of clay-bound boulders, generally steeper on one side than the other, created by the reaction of an advancing glacier with a soft shale bedrock. Much of the surrounding topography is also glacial in origin; there are kames, moundlike hills of sand and gravel deposited near the terminus of a glacier; eskers, low snaking ridges marking the raised courses of meltwater stream-

beds running beneath retreating ice sheets; and of course the ponds and swampy areas left by glacial depression of the land and the diversion of old drainage paths.

This diversity in landforms has led to an equal diversity in plant communities. There are mature, mixed stands of hardwood and evergreens, overgrown meadows, open fields, buttonbush swamp, and even a sphagnum bog — a rarity in southern New England. None of this is surprising, until you get down to some specific plant names — for here are Douglas fir, Korean pine, dwarf Alberta spruce, sweet bay magnolia, amur corktree, mountain laurel, azalea — even sawara cypress. These are things that just don't grow in Massachusetts, unless someone sets them out on the front lawn. Even that explanation will only do for the azaleas and some of the smaller species. But Douglas fir? Whose front lawn was this?

The answer to that question involves a bit of background. The chief Masconomet transferred ownership of the lands along the Agawam (later Ipswich) River to John Winthrop, first governor of the Massachusetts Bay Colony, in 1639. In 1643, 500 acres of this land became the property of Simon Bradstreet, husband of the poet Anne Bradstreet and later Winthrop's successor as governor of the colony. From 1658, the Bradstreets lived in what is now North Andover, and their Topsfield land was leased to a succession of farmers.

Some idea of the bounty that the Bradstreets and their lessees enjoyed is conveyed by one of the governor's heirs, Nathaniel Bradstreet, who wrote that

> in the spring of the year the meadows on the banks of the river were overflowed, so that hundreds of acres were covered with water, making a veritable sea where wild geese and ducks abounded to the delight of sportsmen. Early in the spring the waters would recede and pass out into the ocean through the mouth of the river at Ipswich. There would soon grow up a luxuriant crop of grass on the meadow which, when mature, was grown and harvested.

IPSWICH RIVER WILDLIFE SANCTUARY

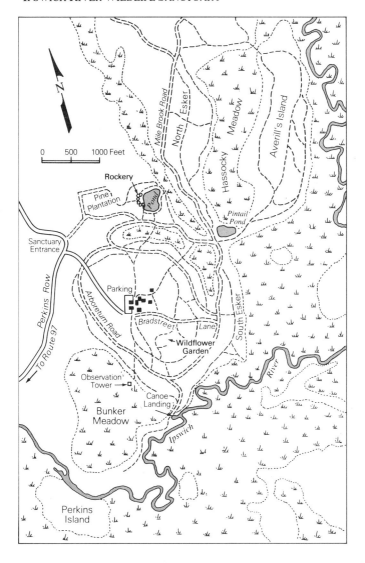

Still, no Douglas firs.

Samuel Bradstreet built the white house, which still stands atop Bradstreet Hill, about 1763. The house and the property surrounding it descended from Bradstreet to Bradstreet until 1898, when Thomas Emerson Proctor purchased it as part of a series of Topsfield and Wenham acquisitions which he combined to form one of the larger North Shore estates of his era. At one time he owned over 4,000 of Topsfield's 8,400 acres.

Thomas Proctor liked to plant things — shrubs, flowers, and especially trees. He wanted to have specimens of all North American tree species growing on and about Bradstreet Hill, but his silvicultural ambitions did not stop at these shores. He acquired dozens of Oriental species, and had them planted on his estate. This is why the native species — though they are slowly but surely reasserting themselves at the expense of the exotics — are nevertheless still interspersed with trees and shrubs which none of the old Bradstreets had ever seen.

Proctor died in 1949, and two years later the Massachusetts Audubon Society purchased the bulk of his estate, adding small adjacent tracts during the succeeding decades. Among the larger of these tracts was some 500 acres of Wenham land donated by Peter Higginson, who had planted an extensive stand of pine.

AUTOMOBILE: Take Route 1 north to Route 97. Turn right and follow 97 to the intersection with Perkins Row. Turn onto Perkins Row and follow signs to the Sanctuary entrance and parking area.

One of the more idiosyncratic and unusual modifications that Thomas Perkins made to his Topsfield barony was the Rockery, which Italian laborers began in 1902 and took nine years to complete. The Rockery, which rambles alongside a nearly hidden pond barely a quarter mile north of the main buildings, was the locus for many of Proctor's exotic plantings, in particular for a profusion of rhododendrons. Audubon's current Ipswich River superintendent Ralph Scott calls the Rockery "North

IPSWICH RIVER WILDLIFE SANCTUARY

America's answer to the pyramids," and even if, like Scott, we keep tongue in cheek, we have to admit that this pile matches anything done at Giza for sheer willfulness, if not in scale.

To look at — and to walk through — the Rockery today, you would think that it had been here for hundreds of years, perhaps even that it was some bizarre antediluvian natural feature of the place. No doubt that is precisely what Proctor had in mind when he had his men haul immense boulders into position to form troughs, steps, ledges, and rustic halls and arches, then festoon them with rhododendron and trailing shrubs so artfully that the hand of man is nearly invisible on casual inspection. If a closer look reveals an Oriental sensibility, that is because much of the project's direction came from the Japanese landscape architect Shintare Anamete. If, instead, you find the overall effect spooky, chances are you have been watching adventure films about lost worlds.

The natural features of the sanctuary are at least as interesting if not as immediately arresting as the Rockery. In addition to Bradstreet Hill, the high ground here consists of the North and South Eskers, extending east and northeast of the hill, and the various "islands" — Averill's, Pine, Perkins, Fowler's — rising out of the marshy lowlands or "meadows" that are so imperfectly drained by the meandering Ipswich River and its tributaries. Perkins Island has nearly a thousand feet of frontage on the river, and is accessible by canoe to campers on a fee and reservation basis (inquire at the sanctuary office for details).

THE WALK: Trails at the Ipswich River Wildlife Sanctuary are clearly marked; major paths along high ground and to the river are indicated on the map on page 7. In addition to the Rockery, note that trails lead along the length of both eskers; to a canoe landing on the river (rentals to members only); to an observation tower on Bunker Meadow; and — just south of Bradstreet Lane, beyond the administration buildings — to a wildflower garden that is at peak bloom in April and early May. There are approximately fifteen miles

IPSWICH RIVER WILDLIFE SANCTUARY

of trails in all. They are nearly as popular with cross-country skiers as they are with summer visitors, even though they are not specially groomed by Audubon.

The Ipswich River Sanctuary incorporates several types of habitat, so it is not surprising that animal species, particularly birds, are correspondingly diverse. The sanctuary is the focus for regular Audubon bird censuses, including a winter count each January and another, conducted via canoe, in mid-June. In addition, there are weekly birding walks on Saturdays in April and May. Two hundred and twenty-one species of birds have been recorded here since 1951; of these, ninety-eight species nested within the sanctuary. One hundred and thirty-five species were counted in 1982 alone; according to Ralph Scott, that is about the number of regularly occurring species that can be depended upon, "regular" referring roughly to two or three sightings of the same species within a five- or six-year period. Among the most unusual sightings in recent years was that of a great gray owl.

The size of the sanctuary, and the relative inaccessibility some of its farther corners, has resulted in the continued presence of a healthy assortment of mammals — twenty-six species, at last count — and reptiles as well. River otter, though uncommon, have been observed on Bunker Meadow, Mile Brook, and in Rockery Pond; other mustelids occasionally reported include long-tailed weasels and mink. Fresh beaver cuttings were seen in 1976, although this animal is not well established here. The opossum, rare at this northern extreme of his territory, has been identified by tracks only.

The white-tailed deer is one species which was once a good deal more abundant in the Ipswich River drainage area; its current rarity, even on sanctuary property, is due to the depredations of dogs allowed to run free.

Seven species of frogs and toads and four of snakes are common at the sanctuary. So are the spotted and red-backed salamanders, although the blue-spotted salamander has gone uncollected since 1976. Snapping and painted turtles are frequently seen, but spotted and musk turtles are regarded as uncommon and the box turtle — unaccounted for since 1977 — is considered rare.

As the presence of muskrats, snapping turtles, wood ducks, great blue herons, and the occasional otter will attest, the river is the dominant feature of the sanctuary. The Ipswich is an old, slow-moving river that rises in the vicinity of Burlington and North Reading. Its course is so convoluted that it wanders through Wenham Swamp and the Audubon property for nearly ten miles, and from there takes another fifteen miles to reach tidewater at Plum Island Sound. The crow would not fly this route.

Wenham Swamp, which characterizes so much of the sanctuary's habitats and in terms of simple acreage comprises so much of its holdings, is the creation of this sluggish river and of its casual regard for its banks, as well as of the poor drainage characteristics of the underlying soil. Concern over the status of the swamp as a viable wetland, and of the survival of such unique features as the six-acre white cedar-sphagnum bog at Cedar Pond in the southeast corner of the sanctuary, has been at the root of opposition to any increase in the volume of water drawn from the Ipswich River by the communities along its course. More than twenty southern Essex cities and towns tap the river for at least part of their water supplies, and several others employ wells drilled directly into the adjacent aquifer. The Massachusetts legislature has authorized a maximum annual Ipswich River draw of seven billion gallons, a figure which has been contended by many environmentalists as unrealistic, particularly during dry years. Measures for improving flow control, thus optimizing the amount of water that could be taken, have been proposed and protested, and it is likely that the controversy will continue well into the foreseeable future.

The Ipswich River Wildlife Sanctuary, Topsfield, Massachusetts, is open year-round. The general admission charge (nonmembers) is $1.50 for adults, $.75 for seniors and children. There is a $1.00 day-use fee for nonmembers entering the sanctuary by canoe. For further information, call 887-9264.

2

BELLE ISLE MARSH

Walking — a living salt marsh, and one of the area's best birding spots, within the metropolitan confines of Boston, Winthrop, and Revere. A short walk traverses several plant communities, which illustrate the continued viability of this fertile and incongruous environment.

WHEN THE ARBELLA and its sister ships delivered the founders of Boston to the Shawmut peninsula and environs in 1630, one of the predominant features of the coastal environment was salt marsh. Since then we have learned a great deal — much of it has gone unheeded, to be sure — about the fecundity of salt marshes and their importance as the primary link in the complex marine ecosystem, nurturing the small and simple creatures at the base of the sea's food chain. But consider what a salt marsh meant to people intent in building their "city on a hill," as Governor Winthrop called it, at the estuarial confluence of the Mystic and the Charles. You couldn't dig foundations in it, and you couldn't sail across it to dry land. It was a no man's land, and all reason seemed to suggest that it be filled in.

It was filled in. If you ride a swan boat in Boston's Public Garden, you are splashing across what was once salt marsh at the fringes of Boston Common. The same observation could be made about other inland or coastal places around the city. A far shorter list would be of those quarters in which living salt marshes survive — areas such as the Neponset Reservation, Thompson's Island, and Belle Isle.

Belle Isle Marsh lies in the far northeastern corner of Boston,

extending partially into Winthrop and Revere. It comprises roughly 265 acres. Survival of such a large block of relatively undisturbed marshland has been one of those urban accidents, in which development was postponed or simply not thought of before the new environmental consciousness of the late sixties began to take hold. Not that there have never been any encroachments or threats — part of the open higher ground adjacent to the marsh along Bennington Street was once a drive-in theater, most vestiges of which have now disappeared; and various legal battles over proposals ranging from housing to cemeteries have kept the marsh's partisans on their toes. (The principal organization working on behalf of the area is the Friends of Belle Isle Marsh, of whom more below.)

Part of the protectionists' problems have stemmed from the disparate nature of ownership of Belle Isle Marsh. Forty-eight acres lie in Winthrop; of these, twenty-three acres are private and twenty-five are designated as conservation land, subject to Winthrop Conservation Commission restrictions. Another twenty-nine-plus acres are in Revere — about seven of these are privately held, and the remaining acreage belongs to the city of Revere and the state. The rest of Belle Isle Marsh is in Boston. A description of jurisdictions here would be somewhat complicated; basically, most of the Boston section was owned by the Massachusetts Port Authority but has been placed under the "care and concern" of the Metropolitan District Commission (MDC). Several years ago, the MDC set about making the East Boston section into a park, a process which involved taking the drive-in theater by eminent domain. Funding shortages have so far kept the park from being completed, but when it is, it will occupy the higher and drier sections of the tract, providing a pleasant, naturally landscaped buffer for the marsh proper.

PUBLIC TRANSPORTATION: The newest station on the MBTA's Blue Line is Suffolk Downs, on Bennington Street near the racetrack of the same name. This stop provides the most direct access to Belle Isle; you may enter the marsh via

Belle Isle Marsh

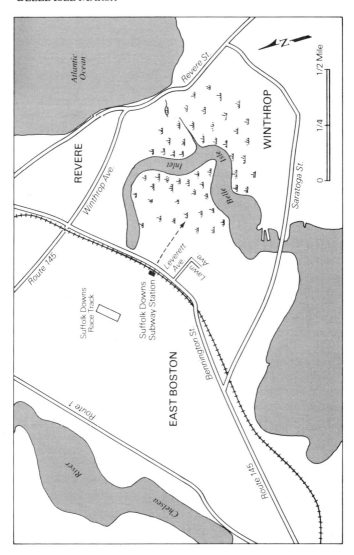

the path alongside the gate almost directly opposite the station. As the park development continues, this gate will be unlocked, and should then be open to vehicles. There will be parking immediately inside the gate.

AUTOMOBILE: Take the Callahan Tunnel from downtown Boston to East Boston. Follow Route 1A north past the Logan Airport access road to Route 145 (Bennington Street), which bears off to the right and continues on to Suffolk Downs. Look for the gate opposite the new Suffolk Downs MBTA station; until better parking accommodations are provided, you may park off the street in front of the gate. If there is no room, backtrack to Leverett Avenue, turn left, and park on one of the side streets.

THE WALK: A visit to Belle Isle Marsh is not so much a matter of following prescribed paths as it is progressing through several stages of plant growth and surface consistency. By putting Bennington Street directly behind you and heading toward the low "skyline" of Winthrop, you will pass through the drier and more elevated parkland to the moist, cushiony grasses of the marsh itself. Note the word moist. Like all salt marshes, Belle Isle is a creature of the tides. During low tide, walking presents less of a problem on the marsh unless you are really intent on getting your feet wet. At or near high tide, rubber boots are a good idea. Have a pair in your car or knapsack anyway, in case you haven't followed the tide tables too closely.

High tide or low, your progress through the marsh will be checked eventually by Belle Isle Inlet, which loops up from the south, ending near Bennington Street at a point to the left of the entrance gate. Given this waterway and the presence of the streets to the west and south, a walk around Belle Isle is easily circumscribed and offers no real directional problems.

BELLE ISLE MARSH

The name Belle Isle — "beautiful island" in French — has been interpreted as an early reference to an upland portion of the marsh, actually a low, gravelly drumlin lightly forested with poplar and quaking aspen, near the end of Leverett Avenue at Lawn Street. It is more likely, though, that the name refers to Orient Heights. Like the Beachmont section of Revere, the Orient Heights part of East Boston is itself a glacial drumlin, formed some 12,000 years ago. Since it was the most prominent of the elevations of dry land that once made up East Boston, Belle Isle more likely refers to Orient Heights than to one of the dozens of inconsequential islands.

All quirks of nomenclature aside, Belle Isle *is* a real salt marsh, its biological processes functioning with remarkable vigor despite its nearness to people, highways, industry, and a major airport. What makes a salt marsh a salt marsh? The foundation of this type of ecosystem is the accumulation of silt which forms at the heads of bays and estuarial mouths over many centuries — silt which eventually turns open water into a mud flat capable of supporting salt-tolerant grasses and other plants. The cycle of death and deterioration of these plants enriches the soil from which they grow, providing nutrients not only for succeeding generations of vegetable life but for plankton and other small marine creatures — such as crustaceans and worms — which in turn feed the young fish that hatch in protected tidal waters. It has been estimated that one acre of healthy salt marsh can engender ten tons of organic matter in a single year. This simple fact, coupled with the indispensability of marine wetlands as flood-preventing "sponges" capable of absorbing huge amounts of excess surface water, makes salt marsh preservation a practical as well as an aesthetic imperative.

The uppermost layer of surface matter at Belle Isle is called, prosaically enough, muck. It is a combination of blue-green algae and the remains of recently dead plants. The action of salt water on this decomposing material is what creates the characteristic sulphur dioxide "rotten egg" smell of the salt marsh, an aroma which is not at all unpleasant once you get used to it. Beneath the muck is a layer of peat, which is nothing more or less than older and more heavily compacted decayed plant matter. The base stratum is the inorganic subsoil known as Boston Blue Clay.

What of the plants themselves? There are a good half-dozen basic salt marsh species, and the presence of most of them at Belle Isle is one of the best indications we have of the system's viability. All are marked by their successful adaptation to inundation by salt water at their roots — remember, twice each day the Atlantic seeps its way into all but the higher reaches of Belle Isle.

Two varieties of *Spartina* thrive here. *Spartina alterniflora* is a tall, spiky grass, while *Spartina patens* grows in flattened clumps which resemble so many cowlicks. One trick to keeping dry here is to step on these clumps of *S. patens* whenever possible, since they keep your feet from penetrating into the muck.

Salicornia is another plant common in healthy salt marshes and related oceanside environments. It grows in little bulbous, reddish-green bunches lying close to the ground; the three different species native to the northeast vary primarily in the length and thickness of their succulent leaves. *Salicornia* is edible, either out-of-hand or in salads. It has a crisp texture and a pleasant salty flavor.

The most highly visible plant at Belle Isle is not a true salt-marsh species at all. It is *Phragmites communis*, the tall, feathery-topped reed familiar along roadsides and in freshwater urban wetlands. *Phragmites* is an incredibly hardy plant that swiftly takes over when conditions no longer favor the more fragile and discriminating marsh grasses. It is therefore a sign of wetlands which have been seriously disturbed by pollution, landfill, or other human encroachment. One thing *Phragmites* cannot abide, though, is salt water. At Belle Isle, the best indication that you are passing from dry land to the tidally influenced salt marsh environment is the abrupt end of the

BELLE ISLE MARSH

march of *Phragmites*. They will grow to the tide line, and no further. Were any of the living marsh to be filled, they would quickly spread their rhizomatous growth to the new limits of tidal seepage. It's no coincidence that the Phragmites line is also the flotsam and jetsam line, since this is the farthest point to which driftwood and less picturesque items are carried by high tides.

Besides distinctive vegetation, there are small-scale topographical features — natural and man-made — peculiar to the salt marsh. Among these are *salt pannes*, miniponds some two to six feet across, some of which can be up to six or eight feet deep. (Don't step in them, rubber boots or no rubber boots.) They are formed when pockets of sulphur dioxide gas lying beneath the surface cause the layers of peat above to collapse. The gas pocket builds up, gives way, and the earth settles, as if the whole process were some sort of terrestrial indigestion. The pan then fills with salt water. If enough of these are created in sequence, they may form a continuous channel leading to open water, thus providing a good, protected place for fish to lay their eggs.

Since nature generally abhors a straight line, we must come up with another explanation for the plumb-true troughs which bisect the marsh at occasional intervals. These are called "mosquito ditches," and they are of course man-made. They were dug as long ago as colonial times, and their exact rationale is no longer clear. Some salt marsh observers feel they were part of an attempt to drain the marshland, thus eliminating a breeding ground for mosquitoes; others suggest that the idea behind them was to create access for fish who would eat the mosquito larvae. Whatever the explanation, they serve to integrate the marsh and marine environments by providing a haven for eels, green crabs, horseshoe crabs, and small fish such as three- and four-spined sticklebacks and mummichogs. Even the jellyfish *Hydra medusa* turns up in the Belle Isle ditches, as do periwinkles, soft shell clams, mud dog whelks, and salt marsh snails.

It is the abundance of bird life at Belle Isle, however, that has

attracted the attention of amateur and professional naturalists and helped to enlist support for the area's continued protection. Because of its food supplies and virtual freedom from predators, Belle Isle is an important stopover on the Atlantic flyway, as any visit during migration seasons will attest. (Early spring and early fall are the best birding seasons at Belle Isle, with the first post-dawn hours the best time of day. The marsh can be hot, sticky, and buggy in summer.) Over two hundred snowy egrets have been seen here in one day. White pelicans and even a bald eagle are among mid-1980s overhead sightings. It is not at all unusual to see blue-winged teal and black-crowned night herons taking cover in the dense stands of *Phragmites* upland from the marsh.

In the winter, Belle Isle hosts a sizeable population of buffleheads, a distinctive black-and-white ocean duck frequently seen in flocks on the surface of the inlet. It's also a major breeding habitat for black ducks, a species whose numbers are diminishing because of crossing with the far more numerous mallards. Species known to breed at Belle Isle also include killdeer, barn swallow, and yellow warbler. Among possible breeders are the spotted sandpiper, green heron, American kestrel, and ring-necked pheasant. Clearly, the marsh is as lively a bird habitat and favored stopover as many more bucolic northeastern locations.

In order to increase public awareness of this fine resource on the periphery of so heavily populated an area, and to study the marsh and continue lobbying for its preservation and sound management, the Friends of Belle Isle Marsh was organized in 1981. Programs include monthly meetings, slide shows, and weekend walks, and membership is open to all — $3.00 per year for individuals, $5.00 for families, and $1.00 for children and seniors. For further information, write the friends at 20 Palermo Street, East Boston, MA 02128.

3

BROOK FARM

Walking — a 2-mile round trip into the hills above the Charles River in West Roxbury, where George Ripley and his associates conducted a famous nineteenth-century experiment in communal living.

THIS IS A SHORT walk and an altogether tame one, contained entirely within an unbuilt section of West Roxbury in the city of Boston. It starts at the margin of an office park and ends in the midst of cemeteries, by way of marshy woods, but it is pleasant enough for all that and has one of the best literary connections of any of the outings in this book. West Roxbury was the site of Brook Farm, the experimental transcendentalist community of the 1840s that attracted the interest of so many of the leading thinkers and writers of the New England renaissance, and which briefly claimed among its members the young Nathaniel Hawthorne. Our office park-to-cemetery trek takes in parts of what was once Brook Farm, and allows us a glimpse of two of the remaining buildings to have been used by the participants in this idealistic and idealized venture.

AUTOMOBILE: From Boston, take Commonwealth Avenue to Newton Centre and turn left on Centre Street. Follow Centre Street past Route 9; shortly after, bear left at the fork onto Winchester Street. Follow Winchester Street to where it ends at Nahanton Street. Turn right. Within a few hundred yards you will see a small office-industrial park on your left (if you cross the Charles River, you've gone too far). Turn into the park and drive to the end of Wells Road.

MORE COUNTRY WALKS

In September of 1836, a group of disaffected and reform-minded Unitarian ministers, along with other liberal intellectuals, began to meet informally for the purpose of discussing not only the newer European philosophical movements but also the ideas of those in their own midst, such as Ralph Waldo Emerson, who talked of the divinity inherent in the human soul and of the spiritually intuitive capacities of human nature. The novel and evanescent mixture of philosophy and theology which Emerson came to represent was given the name transcendentalism, and the group to which he belonged was called, by 1840, the Transcendental Club.

Among the transcendentalists was a Unitarian minister named George Ripley, a native of Greenfield, Massachusetts who held a pastorate in Boston. Ripley was interested in taking the group's ideas out of the drawing room and experimenting to see if this divinely constructed creature, man, might not be capable of achieving a more equitable social order for himself. The vehicle which Ripley chose for these aspirations should be familiar to anyone who has lived through the 1960s: he wished to start a utopian community.

Ripley stated his case to the members of the Transcendental Club late in 1840. He proposed an "Association" — his term — in which members would purchase shares at $500 each. Ownership of a share would entitle a member to voting rights and enrollment of one pupil in the community's school; room and board were to be secured through cooperative labor. There was no problem in defining what form that labor was to take, for Ripley had a farm in mind. The place he had chosen was a 170-acre spread along the Charles River in West Roxbury. The name *Brook Farm* came from a small stream that flowed across the property.

Ripley's plan was simplicity itself. The Association would purchase the farm with its combined shares, and establish itself as a community of equals. Its members would set about practicing husbandry, instructing the young, and engaging in enlightening conversation; in general, they would put into practice a

Brook Farm

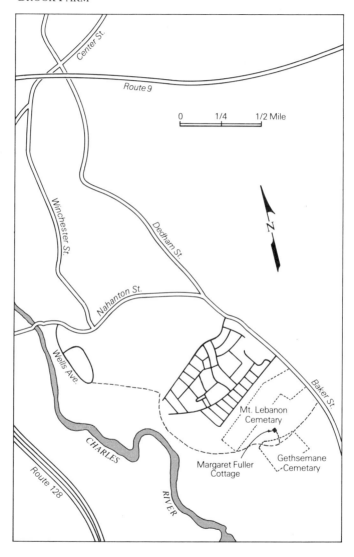

Brook Farm

regimen honest, plain, and rigorous enough to serve as a purgative for the evils and inequities inherent in the false, corrupt, nineteenth-century social order.

Ironically, Ripley's comrades in the Transcendental Club — the very group he would have expected to be most receptive to his idea — did not push each other over in their haste to sign up for Brook Farm. Emerson was one notable holdout; his quarrel with society was that of an individualist, and he saw no reason to trade one confining social structure for another. Nor did Margaret Fuller, the feminist and editor of the transcendentalist magazine, *The Dial*, join in the scheme. Only two members of the Transcendentalist Club, neither of whom were among its founders, cast their lot with the Brook Farm experiment. These were John S. Dwight, a one-time preacher who later turned to music criticism, and Nathaniel Hawthorne, who took $1,000 he had saved while working at the Custom House in Salem and bought shares for himself and his fiance, Sophia Peabody. Brook Farm, the writer hoped, would make a good place for the couple to begin their marriage.

Hawthorne arrived in West Roxbury on April 12, 1841. In those days, what is now the most typically "suburban" of Boston neighborhoods was decidedly rural; Brook Farm itself lay along the road between Dedham and Watertown, and its sole habitation was the old farmhouse which members called the "Hive." (As the community grew, other dwellings and outbuildings were built. The Hive itself stood near the road, now Baker Street, until it was destroyed by fire in 1977.) Hawthorne found about twenty other communalists already in residence. He took his lodgings in the men's dormitory and set about learning the tasks to which he was assigned; this was the young office-worker's first crack at agriculture.

At first, Hawthorne was enthusiastic about his new life and especially about its bucolic setting. "I feel," he wrote to Sophia, "the original Adam reviving in me." As well he should have — this was, after all, in keeping with Ripley's lofty goals. But the prelapsarian Adam lived in Paradise, where the crop yields were no doubt remarkable. Brook Farm, for all its beauty, was not quite so fecund. The topsoil was thin and the land best suited for grazing, with the result that produce had to be bought dearly at the cost of shoveling manure and transporting organically rich marsh mud from the banks of the Charles. By June, Hawthorne was writing Sophia that "it is my opinion . . . that a man's soul may be buried and perish under a dung-heap, or in a furrow of the field, just as well as under a pile of money."

As many as fifty Association members and casually affiliated boarders lived at Brook Farm during Hawthorne's time there. The boarders paid four dollars a week for their keep; the others, Hawthorne included, shared the daily routine of four-thirty A.M. rising, dinner at half-past noon, and bedtime at nine. The romance-writer from Salem did not stay among them for long. From what we can gather it was not the hours or the labor that disillusioned him, but the very nature of community living in such close quarters. As his publisher, James T. Fields, once remarked, "he was a man who had, so to speak, a physical affinity with solitude." "Thou and I must form other plans for ourselves," he wrote to Sophia, "for I can see few or no signs that Providence purposes to give us a home here." By autumn he was merely a boarder at Brook Farm, and by the winter of 1841–42 he had returned to Salem.

Brook Farm survived for six more years. There were financial problems, which led in 1843 to a reorganization in which George Ripley lost influence to Alfred Brisbane, a follower of the French industrial socialist Charles Fourier. As the structure of Brook Farm stiffened into a *phalanx* (the official term for the basic unit in Fourier's proposed new social order), some measure of the original transcendentalist spirit was lost — the contest between individualism and collectivism that had warned off Emerson and Fuller, and most likely Hawthorne as well, became an institutional conundrum. Shortly after their new "phalanstery" — a central meeting house — burned, the remaining members of the Association began to lose interest,

BROOK FARM

and in October of 1847, the Brook Farm experiment came to an end. It was to survive as the inspiration for Hawthorne's *The Blithedale Romance* — and, less directly, for a thousand conversations that began in 1969 with "We'll find a place in Vermont..."

THE WALK: At the end of Wells Road, the main thoroughfare of the office park, is the entrance to the Jordan Furniture Company warehouse parking lot. Park on the side of the road outside the lot, and walk through the gate. At the end of the lot there is a low embankment; near its center a path through the woods begins. Follow this path — according to some accounts, it is the descendant of a trail used by Brook Farm residents — for about 200 yards, until it ends in a T-intersection at a wooden fence beyond which is a paved cul-de-sac with several houses. Now turn right, continuing along a broader dirt trail through second-growth woods.

Near where a view of the Charles opens up to your right, the trail forks. Continue straight ahead. You will soon pass the corner of one cemetery on your left, and immediately after, Gethsemane Cemetery will appear on the right as the path begins to ascend a low hill. Take the path uphill to where it meets a wider path, and then turn right and continue uphill on a paved road through the cemetery. Follow this road over the crest of the hill. On your left will be an old ship's cannon; it was originally part of the armaments of the USS Constitution *and was mounted at Brook Farm in 1932, first in front of the Hive and later in the cemetery.*

Continuing past the cannon, you will see on your right a pink granite boulder with a plaque commemorating the Second Massachusetts Infantry, which drilled here during the Civil War, when the surrounding land was part of Camp Andrew. A dirt road begins on your left at the memorial boulder. Follow this road for a short distance — at its end, opposite a weedy meadow at the top of a hill, stands a

decrepit, boarded-up little house which imagination might allow you to perceive as having been modeled after an English country cottage. This is the Margaret Fuller Cottage.

The Fuller Cottage is curiously named. Although it stood here in the days of Brook Farm, we are assured by Margaret Fuller's biographer, Mason Wade, that it is "the only place where Margaret Fuller did not stay on her visits to the Farm." Wade also claims that Fuller was not the owner of a cow which Hawthorne named the "Transcendental Heifer," leaving us to suspect that the novelist's comic accounts of the animal ("very fractious, and apt to kick over the milk pail") in his letters to Sophia were but puckish and thinly disguised metaphoric references to Fuller herself.

If you continue through the woods behind the Fuller Cottage, heading in the direction of Wohliver Cemetery, you will reach the twenty-foot outcrop of Roxbury puddingstone called Pulpit Rock. It was from this rock that the Reverend John Eliot, the "Apostle to the Indians," preached to his converts in their native tongue during the early 1600s. (Eliot, in fact, even translated the Bible into the local Algonquian language.) Returning from the cottage via the dirt road leading to the Second Infantry Memorial, turn left (at the Memorial) and continue down the cemetery access road to Baker Street. On your left, just before you reach the street, is a white frame building now used by the cemetery maintenance staff that once served as a shop for the Brook Farm community. To return to where you parked, either retrace your route through the cemeteries and woods, or turn left at Baker Street and left again at Nahanton Street. The latter route is somewhat longer. Remember that the cemeteries are closed to visitors after sundown.

4

LYNN WOODS

Walking and ski touring — a circuit of approximately 5 miles through the largest of all the Boston area's city parks, with stops along the way at a pirate's cave and two prominent vantage points.

LYNN, THE OLD SHOE CAPITAL at the foot of the North Shore, might almost be defined as a park with a city attached. Massachusetts has its Metropolitan District Commission and Trustees of Reservations preserves, its state parks and forests and its Audubon sanctuaries, but nowhere does it offer anything so vast in the way of a city park as the Lynn Woods. At nearly 1,800 acres, with another 500 acres of ponds, it is an anomaly, a triumph over the ethos of endless development, and perhaps the greatest local vindication of the late nineteenth-century concern over providing what were invariably called "healthful retreats." (In other words, give the shoe workers some air.)

Lynn was first settled in 1629. From the start, the "Lynn Commons," wild lands on the periphery of the town, were kept as a place where all citizens had the right to cut wood and graze livestock in common. In contradiction of the popular image of New England "commons" as a neat public lawn with a white church standing by, these were uncleared lands. Even after a 1706 division of the town's common lands into private holdings, this territory remained in nearly as wild a state as the first colonists had found it. The "wolf pits" north of Lynn's Walden Pond, some traces of which remain to this day, were dug for the very serious purpose that their name implies.

All through the eighteenth and nineteenth centuries the Lynn Commons (or Lynn Woods, as the area came to be called) stayed wild. New Englanders had a knack for carving farms out of some remarkably unpromising terrain, but this was another story. The usual practice was to take the rocks dug from the fields and build walls, cellars, and maybe an occasional house. In the Lynn Woods, there would have been more walls than fields. In an 1889 letter to the chairman of the Lynn Park Commission, the great landscape architect Frederick Law Olmsted nicely summed up the terrain he had been hired to look over: "it is in a singularly wild, rugged, and rude condition . . . The reason it has been allowed to remain in such a character is found in the outcropping ledges and the boulders and gravel with which its surface is strewn."

By 1881, the Lynn city fathers had decided that the Woods ought once again to revert to public stewardship, not as a resource for firewood (although a plan to recoup costs by selective logging was initially considered, and gathering wood from deadfalls was permitted until recently), but as a city park. Rather than immediately begin purchases and condemnations, though, they launched a phased program that was only quasi-public at its inception. By an act of the state legislature, a seven-man board, the "Trustees of the Free Public Forest," was created to begin acquiring acreage within the woods by purchases and gifts. They were to hold these lands in trust until such time as it was decided they should be formally conveyed to the city, meanwhile beginning the work of building the roads, paths, and bridges that the new park would require. The prime mover in the organization was Cyrus M. Tracy, a Lynn resident who had earlier founded an "Exploring Circle" of like-minded citizens interested in educational rambles through the woods. Tracy's aim was to make Lynn aware that it had at its doorstep "an asylum of inexhaustible pleasures."

In 1890, the lands secured by the Trustees during the preceding decade were officially turned over to the city of Lynn. Using this acreage as a nucleus, the city council voted to exercise the

LYNN WOODS

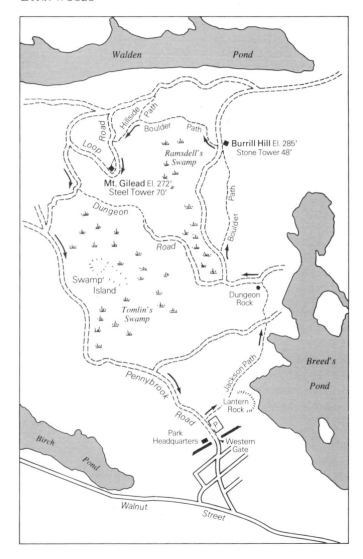

condemnation powers of the state's new park act. Once funds were voted for compensation, the city was able to make the final acquisitions that brought Lynn Woods to its full dimensions.

The Woods were popular from the very beginning, as a look at the 1892 Lynn Park Commissioners' Report will attest. "Our Lynn Woods has created a new world for many of our people," the Commissioners rejoiced. "On fair days in summer, the sight of women and children, with lunch buckets for a day's outing on the shady hillsides of Great Woods roads, tell us how much of a recreation ground Lynn Woods has become." As for the problems of vandalism and visitor comportment — well, there apparently were none: "Those who frequent the Woods seem to have a sense of ownership which begets a feeling of care and responsibility for the property which is better protection than a police, however watchful, could give . . . No complaints of rowdyism and disgraceful conduct have been made. The hoodlum has not yet entered this paradise and no efforts will be spared to keep him out."

That same report regretted that park visitors didn't wander farther from the roads, and "penetrate the depths of the forest." In 1980, something came about which made this a moot point, and brought the entire Lynn Woods far closer to the "wild, rugged, and rude" state which Olmsted had described. This was Proposition 2½, the Massachusetts law which placed a ceiling on property taxes and thus imposed severe constraints on the ability of municipalities to deliver services. In Lynn, the funds required for maintenance of the Woods roads dried up, and all grading and repair operations ceased. The roads have been closed ever since; the Woods remain accessible from the Eastern Gate on Great Woods Road, or the Western Gate at Pennybrook Road (the starting point for our walk, below), but after parking at either of these points an exploration of the vast property must begin on foot or cross-country skis. The impossibility of vehicular travel through the Woods is certainly seen by some to be a blessing in disguise, but it has also brought problems. For one thing, policing is more difficult; for another, whatever "rowdy-

LYNN WOODS

ism and disgraceful conduct" may occur is now more likely to be associated with trail bikes, snowmobiles, and other prohibited off-road vehicles than with conventional automobiles and motorcycles. According to officials, the park is not especially dangerous despite its size and the remoteness of certain sections. As with all of these walks in semiurban places, though, the usual precautions are recommended.

PUBLIC TRANSPORTATION: From Boston, take the Lynn bus out of Haymarket Square, connecting at Central Square, Lynn, with the Number 429 North Saugus bus. The 429 runs along Walnut Street; get off at Pennybrook Road and walk several blocks uphill (to the right of Walnut Street) to the Western Gate of Lynn Woods.

AUTOMOBILE: Take Route 1 north to the exit for Walnut Street, Lynn. Turn right, and follow Walnut Street for about 2 miles (Birch Pond will be on your left). Turn left at the traffic light onto Pennybrook Road, which leads directly into the Western Gate of Lynn Woods.

THE WALK: There is no single recommended course to follow for a walk through Lynn Woods, especially since the roads are clear of traffic, ungraded, and for all practical purposes reverting to trails (this state of affairs will change with an infusion of new money after 1985, but we'll get to that later). The following is one possible circuit, which includes several prominent natural features of the Woods.

Enter the Woods at the Western Gate, on Pennybrook Road. The bungalow on your left, just inside the gate, is the administration building; on weekdays during working hours (the Woods are open daily between sunrise and sunset), you should be able to get a map here. At the end of the parking lot, Jackson Path heads off to the left. On your right is Lantern Rock, an outcropping of felsite overlooking Breed's Pond. Like the other bodies of water in Lynn Woods, Breed's

Pond is part of the municipal water supply. Fishing and swimming are not allowed.

From here the path goes over a hill; on the other side, cross Waycross Road and ascend the stone steps leading to Dungeon Rock.

Dungeon Rock is the focus of one of the innumerable legends of New England pirate treasure, and of one of the even more curious stories of a man's singleminded efforts to get at it. According to old accounts, a buccaneer named Captain Tom Veal came here in 1658, with the British authorities on his heels. He lived in a cave beneath Dungeon Rock, presumably with the horde of treasure with which successful pirates retired in the days before IRAs and Keogh Plans, until an earthquake or rockslide made a deep tomb of his little retreat.

Nearly two hundred years later, a Mr. Hiram Marble of Charlton, Massachusetts, was told by a medium that he was to dig for buried treasure at a place north of Boston. When, in 1852, he heard the story of Veal and his loot, he bought Dungeon Rock from the city of Lynn and started drilling and blasting. He was assisted in this task by another clairvoyant and the spirits she summoned, one of whom was Captain Veal himself. Over the course of eighteen years, Marble and his son Edwin made their way through 200 feet of rock. Upon finding the treasure — which, spirit help notwithstanding, they never did — they planned to donate it to the city so that Dungeon Rock and environs could become a public park. Their wish came true without the windfall, although a few doubloons might have softened the blow of Proposition 2½.

Hiram Marble died in 1868, and Edwin, whose own grave is near Dungeon Rock, continued digging for a few more years. The rock evidently stayed in family hands; when, in 1887, the trustees were acquiring land for the park, a purchase from a Mrs. H.L. Marble was made in this vicinity. In the years since, a good part of the tunnel the Marbles dug has filled up with water, but it is still possible to enter the excavation through an iron door

in a cleft in the rock (on your left, as you approach via the Jackson Path) and descend for a short distance on wooden stairs and along the sloping rock floor. If you try it, bring a powerful flashlight and *be careful. If you explore the cave, you do so completely at your own risk. Neither the Trustees of the Lynn Woods nor the AMC bears any liability.*

Just past Dungeon Rock, Jackson Path meets Dungeon Road. Turn left on Dungeon Road, then right at the next intersecting road. Within a short distance, Boulder Path forks off to the right. It's easy to recognize, as it is bordered with boulders along both sides. Turn onto Boulder Path and follow it as it leads up over a hill, from which you can look ahead to the stone tower atop Burrill Hill. If you look behind you here in winter, you will get your first good views of the ocean.

Continue on Boulder Path to Burrill Hill (285 feet). Like the other prominent hills and outcroppings in the northern part of Lynn Woods, Burrill Hill is largely composed of sienite; most of those to the south, as we saw at Lantern and Dungeon Rocks, are felsite. The stone observation tower on Burrill Hill is closed as of this writing, and it is dangerous to ascend even if you think you can manage it. Best wait; it will likely be repaired and reopened within the next few years.

At the tower, Boulder Path joins a gravel road. The path resumes opposite the tower steps, descending into a glen to the north of Ramsdell's Swamp. Bear left at a fork part way downhill, and continue towards Hillside Path, at which you will again bear left to reach the Loop Road that skirts the foot of Mt. Gilead (272 feet). A short trail heads off to the right and ascends Mt. Gilead, where there is a steel observation tower (no present access). The views of the Boston skyline are particularly fine from this point.

From Mt. Gilead, continue on the Loop Road to the T intersection with Dungeon Road and bear left. This will take you to Pennybrook Road — continue straight at a point

Lynn Woods

where three roads (paths, in their current state of repair) come together. Stay on Pennybrook Road and within a mile or so you will come to the parking lot where you began your circuit of the Woods.

There are changes in store for Lynn Woods. A recent Massachusetts state appropriation of $13 million is to be apportioned among the various parks which Frederick Law Olmsted designed or helped design, and in view of his consulting role in the development of the Woods as a city park, some of that money will be spent here. Regrading and reopening of the roads will be a priority, as will the repair of the two observation towers that you visited on your walk. Work will probably commence in 1985, and will involve an expanded municipal commitment to policing and maintenance along with the projected capital improvements.

This new investment in Lynn Woods has come not a moment too soon. If properly applied, it will prove that we have at least as much foresight as the author of the Lynn Park Commissioners' 1891 report, which stated that "Fifty years hence the population within a radius of ten miles of Boston, if the present rate of increase of large towns continues, will number not less than 3,000,000. These forest spaces for air and exercise which can be provided today at such a trifling cost, will be of inestimable value to the large population which will seek relaxation and rest in Lynn Woods."

5

MOOSE HILL WILDLIFE SANCTUARY

Walking and ski touring — several miles of trails crisscross a small but ecologically varied Massachusetts Audubon Sanctuary in suburban Canton. Nearby is an interesting museum devoted entirely to whaling.

MOOSE HILL WAS THE FIRST of the Massachusetts Audubon Society's wildlife sanctuaries, and it is one of the oldest in the United States. The Society itself was formed in 1896 (it is a separate institution from the national Audubon Society) and today has grown to encompass seventeen sanctuaries with a total acreage of 17,000. But until 1916, all of Massachusetts Audubon's activities were educational; no investment had yet been made in property to be used for preservation and interpretation.

In that year, Dr. George W. Field, then Massachusetts commissioner of fisheries and game, offered Audubon his 225-acre estate in Sharon for use as a bird sanctuary. The estate, which in those days still wore the appearance of a nineteenth-century farm rather than a twentieth-century second-growth woodland, came along with a colonial farmhouse in which Audubon set up its first field office and visitors' center. In June of 1918 the Society hired the ornithologist Harry G. Higbee as resident warden at this first Moose Hill Sanctuary, and the start of Higbee's tenure on the property is generally regarded as the beginning of Mass. Audubon's commitment to employing the sanctuary system as a vehicle for both environmental preservation and public education. As stated in its 1921 annual report, "The Society's aim in this work is to show how birds may best

be attracted to any farm or estate, to so attract and protect them over a large area and especially to make the place so interesting to the general public that it will make pilgrimage to it and learn the methods employed."

The Field farmhouse, with Higbee in residence, would probably seem to the modern visitor to be a fair prototype of today's Audubon reception facilities. There was a display of the Society's literature, as well as Higbee's own mounted collections of birds, insects, flowers, and minerals. Moose Hill was a popular place; in 1920, there were over 2,600 visitors to the sanctuary, and they came from as far as Cuba, Great Britain, and Japan. If the number does not seem impressive in the light of today's sanctuary use figures (Audubon's big Ipswich River Wildlife Sanctuary draws some 75,000 visitors each year), remember that neither publicity nor personal transportation were then what they are today, and that the very idea of a publicly accessible wildlife preserve was still a relatively new one.

Within five years, Audubon's Sharon property came to include 900 acres of the then completely rural town. By 1922, for reasons which the records do not make entirely clear, it became necessary for the Society to leave its sanctuary headquarters in the old farmhouse on the Field property (eventually, that property itself passed out of Audubon's hands and is not now a part of the Moose Hill Sanctuary).

But in that same year, 1922, Mass. Audubon bought a nearby 45-acre tract from Frederick Briggs which also had a house that could be used for the warden's quarters and visitors' center, and which today forms the core of the Society's 227-acre Sharon holdings. The price of this land — all 45 acres, including the house and outbuildings — was $8,000.

AUTOMOBILE: Take Route 1 south from Boston to Route 27 in Walpole. Head east (left) on 27 and continue for just under ¼ mile, then turn right onto Moose Hill Street. Follow Moose Hill Street for 1½ miles to the Sanctuary entrance and parking area.

MOOSE HILL WILDLIFE SANCTUARY

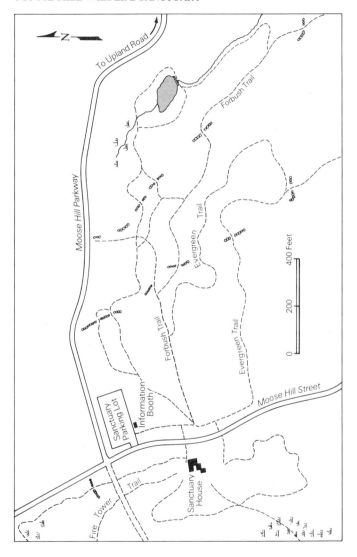

The topography of Moose Hill, and the biological communities which inhabit it, make up a fine representative slice of the inland Massachusetts coastal plain environment. The property extends from the top of Moose Hill down through second- and third-growth hardwood forests to the ponds and marshes east of the summit near Moose Hill Parkway.

Moose Hill itself is a formation of Dedham Granodiorite, a metamorphic rock some 350 million years old. Uplift of the bedrock base and erosion of the softer surficial rock that surrounded Moose Hill eventually made it higher than the neighboring terrain. The present outline of the hill reveals the northwest-to-southeast course taken by the Wisconsin ice sheet, which scoured southeastern Massachusetts as recently as 12,000 years ago. The northwestern slopes of the hill, which were the first to meet the advancing glacier, rise smoothly and gradually. On its opposite side, though, Moose Hill shows the effects of the glacier's continued advance once this obstacle was behind it — the "plucking" of boulders, loose pockets of gravel, and fragments of exposed bedrock from the hill face by a mass of ice that was now pulling rather than pushing its way past.

The area below Moose Hill — those parts of the sanctuary that lie to the east of Moose Hill Street — also show evidence of the glacier's having come and gone. Eskers were formed as gravel accumulated in the beds of glacial meltwater streams (see Chapter 1, Ipswich River Wildlife Sanctuary); there is a vestige of one on the right-hand side of Moose Hill Sanctuary's Forbush Trail as you head south towards the Big Pine Trail. Ponds and marshes at Moose Hill (there is a small pond at a fork in the Meadowbrook Trail) are of glacial origin. They mark spots where huge chunks of ice, separated from the main body of the retreating glacier and buried in gravel and debris carried by meltwater, thawed slowly and left hollows that became the ponds of our warmer era. Hence the terms *ice-block* and *kettle hole* ponds. When the zone of saturation — that underground stratum whose upper boundary is called the *water table* — rises

MOOSE HILL WILDLIFE SANCTUARY

to a higher level than the bottom of one of these glacial kettle holes, the hole fills with water and we have our pond. If the depression penetrates to the water table but no deeper, as in a lake in its last stages of sedimentation, the result is a marsh or swamp.

The Moose Hill Sanctuary's abundance of plant species is in large part the gift of its varied topography. Between 400 and 500 species of wildflowers — among them black-eyed Susans, Queen Anne's lace, orange and yellow hawkweeds, daisies, clover, purple-fringed orchids, blue flags, and turtleheads — have been recorded in Sharon, along with 27 species of ferns. The glacially plucked southeastern slopes of Moose Hill offer the shady ledges and good drainage favored by some species, while conditions in the swampy lowlands assure the proliferation of others. In general, the higher elevations that characterize Sharon and distinguish it from its suburban neighbors make possible the plentiful growth there of some northern New England species such as yellow and white birch, which are rare in neighboring towns.

THE WALK: There are trails leading from both sides of Moose Hill Street at the Sanctuary headquarters and information center. The Fire Tower Trail is the route to the summit of Moose Hill; it branches off to the right from the Tree Trail just behind the headquarters house. The distance to the summit from here is between ¼ and ⅓ mile. A new, 600-foot boardwalk also leads from behind the house into an overgrown upland meadow.

An extensive system of trails (chief among them the Forbush Trail) threads through the woods on the opposite side of Moose Hill Street. As of this writing, a program of trail clearing, abandonment, and rerouting makes specific instructions difficult; the best advice is to ask at headquarters or the information booth adjacent to the parking area for the most recent copy of the Sanctuary map.

Note: Moose Hill Sanctuary is on the route of the Warner

Moose Hill Wildlife Sanctuary

Trail, a 34-mile route extending largely through backcountry from Canton, Massachusetts, to Diamond Hill, Rhode Island. The Warner Trail enters the Sanctuary near the intersection of Moose Hill Parkway and Upland Road, and follows both the Forbush and Fire Tower Trails within the Audubon property and over the summit of Moose Hill. It is blazed with white dots and/or unpainted stainless steel discs. The distance from the Canton Junction railroad station (where the Warner Trail begins) to the summit of Moose Hill is 7.3 miles.

Moose Hill Wildlife Sanctuary, 300 Moose Hill Street, Sharon, MA 02067, is open all year, every day except Monday, from 8 to 6. A modest fee is charged for nonmembers. A wide range of Sanctuary programs includes the Moose Hill Day Camp, tours (by reservation) for organized groups, volunteer trail maintenance, and seasonally oriented natural history walks and birding forays.

Visitors to Sharon might be interested to learn that the town is also the home of the Kendall Whaling Museum, which is just a short drive from the Moose Hill Sanctuary. The museum's nine galleries exhibit paintings, whaling gear, scrimshaw, photographs, whaleboats, ships' figureheads, and other artifacts relating to the history of the industry once so heavily dominated by New Englanders. The Kendall Museum is open Tuesday through Friday from 1 to 4; Saturday from 10 to 4. Admission is $1.00 for adults, $.50 for children.

To reach the Kendall Whaling Museum from Moose Hill Sanctuary, take Moose Hill Parkway, which begins near the parking area at the intersection with Moose Hill Street, and continue to Upland Road. Turn left on Upland Road and watch for the Everett Street turnoff; the museum is at the end of Everett Street.

6

LOVELLS AND GALLOPS ISLANDS

Walking — two of Boston Harbor's smaller islands, now a part of a state park, offer camping, walks through woods and meadows, and a look at military ruins, all within a short boat trip and "water taxi" ride from downtown.

OF THE MORE THAN two dozen islands in Boston harbor, the most familiar to both natives and visitors is Georges, site of the brooding, partially restored Fort Warren of Civil War fame. In the original *Country Walks Near Boston*, Alan Fisher profiled Georges Island, just then becoming the nucleus of the new Boston Harbor Islands State Park. Since the publication of that book, work on the park has continued, and several of the smaller, less heavily used islands are becoming increasingly popular day-trip destinations. In this chapter and the next, we'll take a look at several of these lesser islands as well as little-known Peddocks, the largest of them all.

Lovells and Gallops Islands are a natural pair — or more precisely, part of the three-island cluster which includes Georges. They share similar checkered pasts, having experienced, like so many of the other harbor islands, the vicissitudes of war, shipwreck, and pestilence before going into genteel retirement as retreats for campers and hikers. Lovells and Gallops also share one of the more bizarre military installations of Boston harbor — a tunnel, now caved in and inaccessible, which extended beneath the ocean floor from one island to the other. In his 1971 edition of *The Islands of Boston Harbor*, Edward Rowe Snow told how to crawl part way through the

tunnel starting at its entrance on Lovells Island, an entrance now sealed over. He also remarked that no one still knew the history of the tunnel, although Emily and David Kales, in *All About the Boston Harbor Islands*, claim that it was part of post-Civil War construction and was designed to be loaded with explosives, with which to blow up any enemy ship that might attempt to pass through the channel between the two islands into Boston's inner harbor. Rather a lot of civil engineering work, it would seem, for a one-shot deal.

> *PUBLIC TRANSPORTATION: Three boat lines connect downtown Boston with Georges Island. Mass Bay Lines operates from Rowe's Wharf, and Bay State Spray/Provincetown Lines and Boston Harbor Cruises use Long Wharf. Schedules for these lines vary, although daily service usually extends between June and Labor Day, with weekend trips available through Columbus Day. As of this writing, the fare is $3.00 round trip for adults, $2.00 for children and seniors. Once you are on Georges, you can take the free water taxi to Lovells and Gallops as well as to Grape, Bumpkin, and Peddocks Islands (see following chapter). This service operates daily during July and August, with weekend trips to Gallops during June and September.*
>
> *During the rest of the year, the islands are accessible by private boat for day use only (10 A.M. to 6 P.M.).*

Lovells Island, a mixed environment of sand and gravel beaches, wooded hills, and wetlands, covers roughly sixty-two acres. By 1636 it already had its name, after William Lovell of Dorchester. For most of the next two centuries it was used for agriculture, although the earliest records show that it was first granted to Charlestown for use as a fishing station. This is easily understandable; what is not so easy to fathom is why, in the earliest days of settlement, so many of these islands were farmed. There was no shortage of acreage on the mainland, and, after the first few years, the safety from Indians that islands

LOVELLS AND GALLOPS ISLANDS

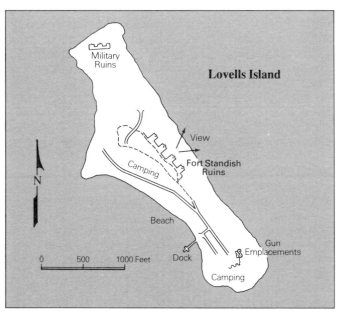

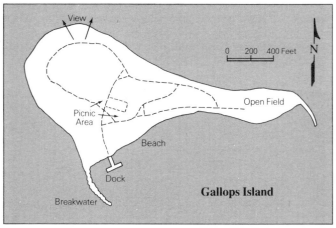

MORE COUNTRY WALKS

afforded was no longer a real necessity. We can only assume that in those days, as now, there seemed something right and cozy about an island — some special attraction that worked its way with those singularly practical first Bostonians, even as it does with us today.

Like many of the other harbor islands, Lovells was drafted into military service. This happened in 1900, with the establishment of Fort Standish. The fort was built because Boston had felt vulnerable to enemy attack during the Spanish-American War (a bombardment by the Spanish fleet had actually been anticipated), but it assumed no real importance until World War II, when many hundreds of soldiers were stationed there. The remains of gun emplacements — the twin concrete circles at the crest of the hill opposite the landing dock — and observation bunkers are reminders of a time when defending the home shores involved scanning the seas for U-boats rather than monitoring computers that might warn of incoming missiles. We tend to forget that the two eras were separated by less than twenty years.

Fort Standish was decommissioned after the war, and Lovells Island lay largely idle until the state park was established. Today there is a new docking facility, and also a swimming beach with lifeguard, trails, guided walk programs, and campsites.

THE WALK: Trails lead directly inland from the dock; the campsites are off to the right near some abandoned bunkers. Follow the trail across the island to the above-mentioned gun emplacement ruins for good views of the outer harbor and its islands. The lighthouse to the left, on The Graves (romantic suggestions of shipwreck and high adventure notwithstanding, "Graves" is after Thomas Graves, a Winthrop sea captain), is Graves Light; on the right is Boston Light, on Great Brewster Island. Paths also lead to the hillier, more heavily wooded northern end of the island, to the left of the gun emplacements as you look towards the outer harbor. Beyond this rise of land the island gets boggy, and then

culminates in a wooded rise of land at the northern tip. A rocky beach extends around this point to the outer, eastern shore.

Gallops Island is much smaller than Lovells — only sixteen acres — and has no camping facilities. Its self-guided trails are, however, good for at least an hour's exploring as they wind through meadows and dense stands of the islands' ubiquitous sumac, past several crumbling reminders of yet another temporary military colonization.

Gallops Island was named for a Captain John Gallop. In his 1649 will, this portion of his holdings was valued at $75 — a matter not so much of islands being worth less then, but of dollars being worth more. For two hundred years Gallops was farmed, and in the 1830s the widow of the last farmer, Margaret Newcomb, opened an inn there that became popular for its home cooking under her management and that of a subsequent owner. By the time of the Civil War the city of Boston owned the island and made it available to the Union Army for quartering troops.

Between 1866 and 1917, Gallops Island was the site of a quarantine station run first by the city and finally by the federal government. Some 250 of those whose illnesses proved fatal are buried here. After the U.S. entry into World War I, Gallops became the place of internment for German merchant sailors who had been on ships in Boston harbor at the time that war between the two countries was declared. During World War II, a radio operators' school run by the U.S. Maritime Service brought hundreds of military personnel to Gallops Island. The buildings they occupied are gone now — dismantled after this last active episode in the island's history — but you will see a number of crumbling foundations as you walk around the island.

THE WALK: The trail leading from the landing divides a short way inland. The path leading to the right parallels the beach (no lifeguard) and continues east to an open field near the breakwater. If you continue straight ahead past the picnic

LOVELLS AND GALLOPS ISLANDS

area (see map), you will pass through thickets of sumac and wild roses and ascend a gentle knoll which commands a fine panorama of the city and harbor. Looking from west to east (left to right) on the high ground, you will see Long Island, with Spectacle Island beyond; the Boston skyline; the control tower of Logan Airport; the black-and-white concrete pyramid which marks the nearly disappeared mini-island of Nix's Mate (once the site of a gallows for pirates); the southern tip of Deer Island and its house of correction; the shores of Winthrop (and, on a clear day, Nahant); Lovells Island in the foreground and the outer islands in the distance; and finally Georges Island (foreground) and the tip of the Hull peninsula at the extreme right. That is the stationary view. You may also see large tankers and freighters passing close by between Gallops and Lovells Islands. This narrow channel is part of the main harbor roads, just as it was when the old tunnel was built and packed with dynamite.

The Boston Harbor Islands State Park is headquartered at 349 Lincoln Street, Building 45, Hingham, MA 02043. Call 617-749-0051 for information. For reservations and permits for camping on Lovells Island, which though part of the state park, is managed by the Metropolitan District Commission, contact the MDC at 20 Somerset Street, Boston, MA 02108 (617-727-5250). Camping permits cost $5.00 per night.

7

PEDDOCKS, BUMPKIN, AND GRAPE ISLANDS

Walking and (on Peddocks) ski touring — three more of the harbor islands, including the largest, a place of abandoned barracks dating from the era of the Spanish-American War, forested drumlins, salt marshes, and meandering pathways.

THIS CONTINUATION OF our exploration of the Boston Harbor Islands brings us into Hingham Bay. We'll visit two islands, each with its own distinctive past and a future tied to public recreation rather than soldiery, sanitariums, or sewage. Like Gallops and Lovells, Peddocks, Bumpkin, and Grape Islands are now all easily accessible from Boston, yet provide opportunities for hikers and campers that are totally incongruous with their proximity to downtown.

PUBLIC TRANSPORTATION: See the preceding chapter for details of connections between downtown Boston and Georges Island. From Georges, the water taxi serves Bumpkin, Grape, and Peddocks Islands. More direct service to Peddocks is provided by Bay State Spray Lines from Boston or Hull (this is the Nantasket boat) or by the commuter boat Gracious Lady, *which operates between Hingham and Boston and stops at Peddocks on request.*

To many people who pass by on boats, or who look down from the sky as their planes make the approach to Logan Air-

port, Peddocks seems the most mysterious of all the harbor islands. It is big — 185 acres covering five glacial drumlins with their connecting lowlands and salt marshes — and, unlike the other islands, heavily wooded. Looming amidst the trees on the easternmost hill is a row of somber, red brick buildings, and near the landing is a white clapboard church. Is this some forgotten Boston neighborhood, isolated from the mainland?

If Peddocks is a "neighborhood," it is probably Boston's least heavily populated. In recent years, the only inhabitants have been an MDC (Metropolitan District Commission) caretaker and his family, and a score or so of summer people who lease the cottages on Central Hill. As with all the harbor islands, the population of Peddocks is more spectral than corporeal. This may well change, though, with a vigorous new recreation and education program being implemented by the Peddocks Island Trust.

Peddocks Island, only a quarter mile across Hull Gut from the Nantasket peninsula, was made a part of Nantasket when the first island settlers crossed the Gut in 1641. It was named for one Leonard Peddock, about whom little is known — including whether he ever lived on the island. Throughout colonial times Peddocks was farmed, the land having been distributed to the yeomen of Hull on the basis of four island acres for every two acres already held on the mainland. During the Revolution, Peddocks was raided by rebel forces on provisioning forays. They took 500 sheep and 30 cattle, from which we can surmise that the heavy stands of maple, birch, and pine which crowd the island today must have been absent with so many grazing animals around.

By the late nineteenth century, Peddocks Island was the property of Mrs. Eliza Andrew, widow of John Andrew, governor of Massachusetts during the Civil War. It was she who deeded eighty-eight acres of the island to the U.S. government for use as a military installation. Like Fort Standish on Lovells Island, the fortifications on Peddocks Island were deemed immediately necessary because of the Spanish threat, although a

PEDDOCKS, BUMPKIN, AND GRAPE ISLANDS

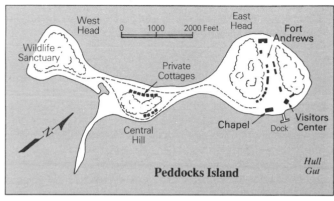

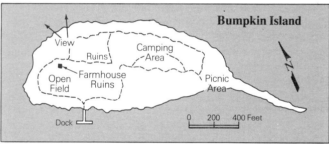

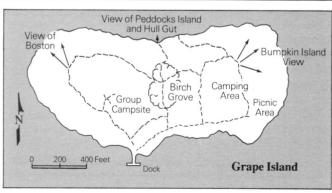

longer-range strengthening of coastal defenses was also part of the plan. It was a military buildup, McKinley-style.

Fort Andrews was dedicated early in 1900. Note the spelling: it was named not for Governor Andrew, but for a Civil War general named Leonard Andrews. The brick buildings which stand so prominently on the East Head today, along with smaller decrepit structures set back farther in the woods, are what remains of the barracks, officers' quarters, and other fort facilities. The church, of course, was the fort's chapel. It is still used occasionally and registered two marriages in 1983.

During the First World War, Fort Andrews bristled with big guns aimed out to sea; the next global conflict saw a greater concern for antiaircraft defenses and radar observation. Peddocks Island was also the place of internment for Italian prisoners taken in World War II. After the war, the POWs were repatriated and the fort, which had been manned by a force of as many as 2,000, was decommissioned. Peddocks was left to its handful of cottagers, and to the triumphant return of its dense vegetation.

At the time that the Boston Harbor Islands State Park was being formed, a number of people concluded that plans more ambitious than the normal provisions for swimming and camping might be in order for this largest of the islands. Accordingly, the Peddocks Island Trust came into being. The Trust, which leases the island from the MDC, is made up of representatives from the New England Aquarium, Tufts University, the Children's Museum, and the Boston Educational Marine Exchange. Its board of twenty-four members is charged with developing ideas for island facilities and uses, many of which are already taking shape.

The Trust has welcomed many summer campers, and has sponsored various nature and history tours. (If you come to stay for a while, you may even be invited to help work on restoring some of the old fort buildings.) Between mid-April and mid-June, over 2,000 students and teachers are ferried to the island for informative day-hikes. Within the next few summers, trails

PEDDOCKS, BUMPKIN, AND GRAPE ISLANDS

will be improved (and new ones blazed), and Community Boating, famous for its Charles River sailing instruction and rentals, will set up a boating camp at Peddocks.

Looking a little further into the future, Trust officials hope to provide youth hostel facilities in part of the old fort, with another building slated for conversion to a country inn with twenty-two rooms. The old fort hospital is the focus of a proposal for an arts center in which artists would have both living quarters and studio space.

Peddocks is the only harbor island open and accessible by boat throughout the year. The taxis from Georges Island run on weekends from Memorial Day through Columbus Day, and weekdays from July 1 through Labor Day. During the off-season, there are periodic group outings scheduled by the Peddocks Island Trust (see below). Among the winter activities scheduled in recent years have been cross-country ski trips sponsored jointly by the Trust and the Appalachian Mountain Club.

In summer, campers find that Peddocks makes an ideal base for exploring other nearby harbor islands (especially Bumpkin and Grape, below) via water taxi, and for excursions to Nantasket Beach — the boat to Nantasket leaves each day at 11 A.M. and returns at 3:30 P.M.

For information on Peddocks Island activities, and for camping permits, contact the Peddocks Island Trust, Old City Hall, 45 School Street, Boston, MA 02108 (523-1184). As of this writing, fees for day use are $2.00 for adults, and $1.00 for children.

THE WALK: If you are not on a guided tour of the island, you can begin your walk at the boat dock and head inland and uphill past the old fort buildings. Don't go inside the buildings because the porches, stairs, and floors are rotten and can easily break through. At the crest of the hill on East Head, bear left on any of the trails to reach Central Hill, where the summer colony is located. Remember that the

leaseholders' cottages are private property, and avoid trespassing in front yards. Admittedly, it is hard to tell where yards leave off and trails begin, since there are no curbstones, paved roads, or vehicles here.

Central Hill is where you begin to notice that Peddocks is indeed an island of changing faces. From the deep, inland-New England forest landscapes in the vicinity of the fort, you will have passed into an area more reminiscent of parts of Cape Cod or New York's Fire Island; elsewhere, parts of the island may remind you of coastal Maine.

The trail descends from Central Hill along the edge of a salt marsh, eventually reaching the westernmost and least developed drumlin, West Head. The brush and trees are at their densest here. In the midst of one of these thickets is one of only two known black-crowned night heron rookeries in Massachusetts — the nests are there, although no birds have been seen in recent years. Bird habitat restoration, incidentally, is one of the Trust's priorities for the western reaches of Peddocks Island.

Bumpkin Island is much smaller — only thirty-five acres — and is much more easily encompassed in a trip of an hour or two. Only several hundred yards from the mainland of the Hull peninsula, it was owned in the seventeenth century by Samuel Ward, who willed it to Harvard College in 1682. Harvard, in turn, leased the island to farmers until the turn of the present century, when Clarence Burrage took a 500-year lease and built a hospital for paraplegic children. The hospital opened in 1902, and operated successfully until the U.S. Navy appropriated the island in 1917. The Navy promptly moved in 1,300 sailors and built over fifty new buildings, and just as quickly decamped and dismantled the base when the First World War ended, barely eighteen months later. The hospital never reopened, and its buildings burned in 1945. You can see the foundation ruins to this day, along with the ruins of a much older stone farmhouse.

MORE COUNTRY WALKS

THE WALK: A path leads directly inland from the boat dock and soon forks to the left and right. Go right to reach the campground and picnic area (for information on camping permits here and on Grape Island, see the preceding chapter). If you turn left, passing some nondescript concrete military ruins, you will head uphill past the farmhouse ruins (right) to a fork. The path to your left offers good Boston skyline views; the right-hand path more clearly skirts the ruins and cellar holes of the hospital. The paths rejoin after a short distance and continue through sumac and aspen stands (watch out for poison ivy) to the camping and picnic areas. From here, you can finish the loop back to the boat dock.

Grape Island is the southernmost of the large islands of Hingham harbor; in fact, it was joined to the mainland as recently as colonial times by a sand spit exposed at low tide. This land access made the island more convenient to farm and to use for grazing, and that is just what the landholders of the seventeenth and eighteenth centuries did. We know that in 1775 a crop of hay was growing on the island, because that spring the Tory who owned it invited some of the British officers from the Boston garrison (this was before the evacuation) to come down and help themselves to it, hay for horses being scarce in the besieged city. According to harbor islands authority Edward Rowe Snow, the British foray was broken up by South Shore minutemen in a fracas grandiloquently remembered as the Battle of Grape Island.

The only other Grape Island story of note, also recounted by Snow, concerns a reclusive ex-slave-trader and smuggler named Amos Pendleton (a.k.a. "Captain Smith") who lived here for a quarter century after the Civil War. The old captain used to fire shots, which may or may not have been warnings, at anyone who set foot on his island.

Grape Island got its name from the wild grapes that grew there in the days of the first settlers, but you won't find any grapes there now (Great Brewster, of all the harbor islands, has the

Peddocks, Bumpkin, and Grape Islands

most wild grapes). Instead there are sumac, blackberries and raspberries, and a profusion of wild roses. A birch grove, near the center of the island, is an unusual feature. Not long ago, you would have been as likely to have rabbits crossing your path on Grape as on any of the harbor islands, but illegal hunting has brought the population way down.

THE WALK: Grape Island's trails lead past no old ruins or other historical curiosities, but for sheer pastoral beauty they are the equal of any of the harbor's pathways. Several trails lead off from the boat dock. Head to the left to reach the group campsite and a hilltop view of Boston. To the right is a trail leading to the ten individual campsites and the picnic area. Before reaching the campsites, turn left to bisect the island by way of the birch grove. The view from the other side is of Peddocks Island (tiny Sheep Island is in the foreground), Hull Gut, and the tip of the Hull peninsula. From the northeastern tip of the island, at the edge of the camping area, you can look across to Bumpkin Island.

8

RAVENSWOOD PARK

Walking and ski touring — a rocky, hilly, heavily wooded 500-acre preserve at Gloucester's western threshhold, laced with miles of trails and eighteenth-century dirt roads. A short side trip takes you to the famous Hammond Castle Museum.

CAPE ANN IS THE WEATHERED prow of the North Shore, its cutting edge in geographic if not — as some south-of-Ipswich chauvinists would have us believe — in social terms. But Cape Ann is also a point of demarcation in the surface geology of the Massachusetts coast. Along its southern exposure to the Atlantic, and east of Annisquam along its northern shores, the cape is made of granite, as the very name "Rockport" will attest. Beyond Annisquam, as the shoreline arcs westward and to the north, the world of salt marshes and barrier dunes begins, yielding again to surf-shattering rock only beyond the Merrimack in New Hampshire and Maine.

The walk in this chapter takes us through Ravenswood Park, set in the heights overlooking the craggy, southerly portions of the Cape Ann shore, where the meeting between land and sea is more abrupt than along the barrier beaches to the north. This is also a part of the world famous for its concentration of the rich and socially prominent during the latter part of the nineteenth and the early part of the twentieth centuries. It was the beneficence of one of those North Shore aristocrats that made possible the preservation of Ravenswood as a park, and the grandiose architectural tastes of another that provides us with an interesting side trip once we've finished our walk.

More Country Walks

Samuel E. Sawyer was a native Gloucesterman, born in 1818. He moved to Boston as a young man and did very well in business there, but he never forgot where he came from. In addition to summering in Gloucester each year of his long life, he made the city the focus of most of his philanthropy. The capstone was the donation, in 1889, of 300 acres of woodland which form the nucleus of Ravenswood Park, along with an endowment that has provided for maintaining and expanding the park (there are now about 500 acres in all) as well as for building a nondenominational chapel near the entrance on Western Avenue (Route 127).

As one of the largest unbroken tracts of forest land in Essex County, Ravenswood Park today is a haven for walkers and cross-country skiers alike. More than five miles of trails provide access to a variety of environments, from a mixed upland forest peppered with huge glacial erratics and broken by outcroppings of the native granite, to a low-lying swamp (to the west of the main entrance road; see walk directions, below) in which the wild magnolia that gives this part of Gloucester its name makes its only Massachusetts stand.

AUTOMOBILE: Take Interstate 95 north to Route 128 north. Take either of the Manchester exits and follow signs to Route 127, which runs through Manchester Center. Head east on 127 into the Magnolia section of Gloucester and watch for the Ravenswood Nondenominational Chapel on your left. The parking lot for Ravenswood Park is adjacent to the chapel. There is space for about ten cars; if the lot is filled, it is usually possible to park on the shoulder near the chapel.

An alternative route, which will let you see more of the old cities of the North Shore as well as its natural features, is to take Route 1A north from Boston to Salem and Beverly (Marblehead is a short side trip on Route 114 just before Salem). Turn right onto Route 127 after crossing the Danvers River into Beverly, and proceed through Manchester as above.

Ravenswood Park

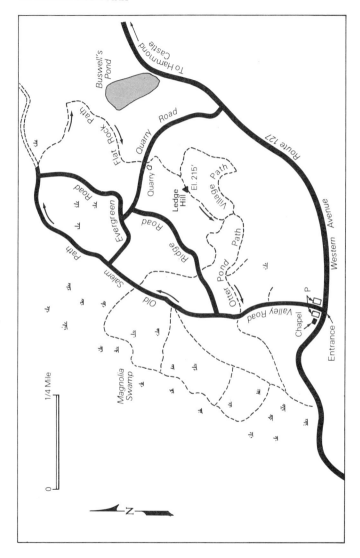

More Country Walks

THE WALK: There are over five miles of trails in Ravenswood Park. The map posted at the parking area (reproduced in this book) will help you plan a route. Keep in mind that the solid lines on the posted map represent broad, well-beaten paths — dirt roads, almost — and that the dotted lines represent trails that are sometimes poorly defined. An exception is the Otter Pond Path past Ledge Hill, which has a stone border for much of its way.

For a good overview of the park's terrain, start out on Valley Road, which extends directly into the park from the parking area. Follow Valley Road past the intersection with Ridge Road on the right, and past the several paths on the left that loop through the periphery of Magnolia Swamp. (If you take any of the swamp paths, bear left after returning to the well traveled and easily identified Valley Road, or, as it is called after the intersection with Ridge Road, Old Salem Path.

Continue on Old Salem Path, through a stand of big white pines around the intersection with Evergreen Road on the right. Near this spot, in the late eighteenth century, there stood a pest house, a place of quarantine for victims of epidemic diseases. No traces appear to remain. Another vanished structure that once stood just ahead to the left on the path was the hut of a hermit named Mason Walton (1838–1917) who wrote prolifically about the life of the forest and entertained frequent guests in a most unhermitlike fashion. At the point ahead where Evergreen Road rejoins Old Salem Path, the path narrows and rises to a broad, flat outcropping of granite which very nearly resembles stone paving. The aptly named Flat Rock Path leads off to the right just beyond this point. Follow Flat Rock Path, keeping a sharp eye out for glimpses of Buswell's Pond to the left. Walk down to the pond, which as of this writing is set in quiet, near-wilderness surroundings reportedly threatened by plans for condominium development along its unprotected eastern shore.

Returning to Flat Rock Path, continue into a shadowy

RAVENSWOOD PARK

stand of eastern hemlock, up a boulder-strewn hill, and across Quarry Road, where there are remnants of old quarrying operations including (adjacent to the path) a low, squared-off boulder marked with drill holes used for blasting. From here, the trail quickly ascends Ledge Hill (215 feet).

From atop Ledge Hill — especially when the trees are not fully in leaf — you can look out across Magnolia and Gloucester Harbor to the mansions of Gloucester's Eastern Point and to the open Atlantic beyond. One of the most beautiful of these mansions is Beauport, maintained by the Society for the Preservation of New England Antiquities and open to the public. To get there, take Route 127 into downtown Gloucester and follow the signs for Eastern Point.

The descent from Ledge Hill should serve as a definitive reason why Gloucestermen turned early to the sea for their living. There are boulders everywhere, a riot of granite, with most of the stones hosting splotches of lichen.

Stay on the trail (from here, it is called the Otter Pond Path, though there is no pond), until you reach Valley Road. Turn left at the road to reach the parking area. (Total distance of loop described is approximately 3½ miles.)

There should still be time, after exploring Ravenswood Park, for a look at one of the North Shore's more famous man-made curiosities. This is the Hammond Castle Museum, popularly known as Hammond Castle.

Continue east (towards Gloucester) on Route 127 after leaving Ravenswood, and turn right onto Hesperus Avenue. The "castle" is on the left about a mile or so down the road. This fanciful structure was built between 1925 and 1928 by John Hays Hammond, Jr., a prolific inventor who pioneered electronic navigational devices. Hammond was rich and able to indulge fantasies that might have earned a poorer man an appel-

lation less kindly than "eccentric." His favorite maxim, it is said, is that one should think in the future, work in the present, and live in the past. His inventions prove his faithfulness to the first two parts of this code, and his house takes care of the rest. It is an agglomeration of authentic period components and reproductions representing virtually every historical aesthetic from the ancient Roman to the Baroque, and its centerpiece is a vast organ, ensconced in its own hall and speaking authoritatively through no fewer than 8,600 pipes.

The Hammond Museum is open every day except Wednesdays and holidays from 10 A.M. to 4 P.M. (Sunday 1 to 4 P.M.). Tours highlight architectural features as well as *objets d'art* from Mr. Hammond's collection. There are frequent concerts on the organ as well as by local chamber groups, and a terrace restaurant is open in the summer. Call 283-2080 for information.

If you go up into the tower of the Hammond Museum and look due south across the Atlantic, you will see, not far from shore, the ancient navigational hazard known as Norman's Woe Rock. This rock may have been the death of many a real-life ship and her sailors, but it is remembered primarily as having caused the fictional wreck of the *Hesperus* in the Longfellow poem. This leaves us with an explanation for the name of Magnolia's main thoroughfare, but not for Norman's identity. Also nearby, and west of the Hammond Museum on Hesperus Avenue, is Rafe's Chasm, a rift in the sixty-foot-high granite cliff that forms the shoreline here. The gap in the rock runs back inland for some two hundred feet. The action and noise of the waves that pierce the chasm might best be appreciated from a vantage point at sea; private property intervenes between the road and the shore, and a close approach on foot is a chancy business.

9

CHARLES W. WARD RESERVATION

Walking and ski touring — a 3-mile ramble through a Trustees of Reservations property that contains both the highest point of Essex County and one of its fascinating low points, a black spruce bog.

THE NORTHWESTERN CORNER of Essex County, along the Merrimack Valley, has seen more than its share of development during the past twenty years. Interstates 93 and 495 have nurtured acres of garden apartments and condominiums called Heritage This and Royal That; at times, it seems as if mock Tudor has taken over as the signature architecture of the place. There is also a plethora of industrial "parks" inhabited by small electronics firms, and giant Western Electric, stepchild of the late Ma Bell, has a vast plant on Route 125 in North Andover near the Haverhill line.

In the midst of all this, it is comforting to find a Trustees of Reservations property that has not only kept a beautiful tract of woodland and meadows open for public enjoyment, but which has actually grown during the four and a half decades since its inception.

The nucleus of the Charles W. Ward Reservation is a farm once owned by Nicholas Holt, Sr., who was among a group from Newbury, Massachusetts who moved inland and in 1646 incorporated the town of Andover. The town then included North Andover as well; in fact, the first settlement was on the site of what is now North Andover Center. Following the custom prevalent in the part of England from which they had

come, the founders of Andover apportioned land in a series of divisions, beginning in the village itself and eventually encompassing the outlying territory. In the fourth division, in 1672, Nicholas Holt acquired the property on Holt Hill around which the Ward Reservation was later created.

Nicholas Holt added acreage to his farm throughout his long life, assuring that his many heirs would have sufficient land to divide after his death. Where there had been one Holt farm there were thus later several, and although some of Nicholas's descendants moved away over the years, at least part of the old family holdings remained under Holt ownership until the 1870s. This last 150-acre parcel changed hands twice during the next forty years, until it was finally purchased by Charles William Ward in 1917. Two years after he bought his retirement farm, Ward made a happy discovery: he was related to the Holts who had originally settled here, and so had inadvertently come into possession of an old family legacy.

Charles W. Ward died in 1933. During the years that followed, his widow, Mabel Brace Ward, learned about the land acquisition and protection activities of the Trustees of Reservations, and decided to donate the family property to the Trustees as a reservation in memory of her late husband. The first transfer, which established the reservation, was made in 1940, but Mrs. Ward continued to purchase and donate surrounding land, so that by the time of her death in 1956 the Trustees' holdings had increased to 273 acres. Expansion of the reservation has continued through the charity and direction of the Wards' grandson, John Kimball, so that some 640 acres are included within its boundaries today.

The Charles W. Ward Reservation encompasses parts of the towns of Andover and North Andover. It extends over three hills — Holt, Shrub, and Boston — and includes meadows kept in hay for harvest, extensive second- and third-growth woodlands, swamp and a small, interesting northern bog area, which we'll explore after making the circuit of the property described below.

WARD RESERVATION

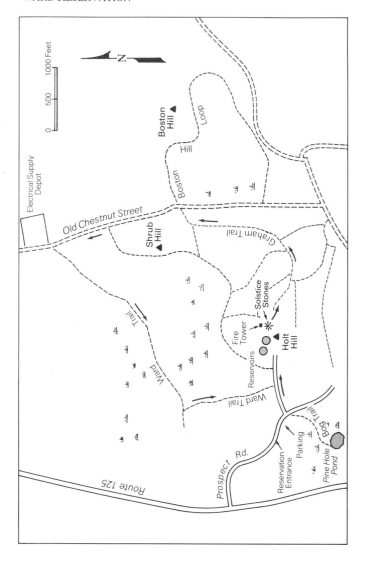

MORE COUNTRY WALKS

AUTOMOBILE: From Boston, take I-93 north to the Route 125 exit. At the exit, take Route 125 north for 5 miles. Turn right onto Prospect Road; you'll see a sign directing you to the Ward Reservation. The reservation parking lot is 0.4 miles ahead of you on the right.

THE WALK: The system of trails at the Ward Reservation is indicated on the map posted at the parking lot; copies are available from the Trustees of Reservations, 224 Adams Street, Milton, MA 02186. Most of the trails connect with the main access road to the Holt reservoirs and fire tower. The following is a suggested route of about 3 miles which offers a representative sampling of the reservation's views and terrain.

Cross Prospect Road at the parking lot and follow the access road uphill to the reservoirs and fire tower. The reservoirs are part of the Andover water supply system; they are situated here because Holt Hill is the highest point in the town and, in fact, in all of Essex County. Rangers from the Massachusetts Department of Natural Resources staff the fire lookout tower during the dry months of the year. On June 17, 1775, Andover farmers and townsmen gathered on top of Holt Hill to watch a different sort of fire: the burning of Charlestown by British troops in the aftermath of the Battle of Bunker Hill.

Near the base of the fire tower is an arrangement of stones set like spokes around a central pair of millstones. These are the "solstice stones." They were the idea of Mabel Brace Ward, who was intrigued by Stonehenge when she visited Britain and began, around 1940, to lay out a pattern of stones which would serve a similar astronomical function. The stones indicate the four main compass points, as well as the points where the sun rises and sets on the longest and shortest days of the year. Sunrise and sunset on the summer solstice are in line with the narrow stones in the northeast and northwest quadrants, respectively; in the winter solstice, the narrow stones in the southeast

WARD RESERVATION

and southwest quadrants line up with the rising and setting sun. At the vernal and autumnal equinoxes, of course, the sun rises and sets along a due east-west line.

To the left of the solstice stones (as you stand with the fire tower behind you and slightly to your left) is an open meadow. Cross the meadow to reach the beginning of the Graham Trail, which winds through the forest for about 0.7 mile before reaching Old Chestnut Street, which is not so much a street as an overgrown eighteenth-century country road, better described as a wide path.

From here you have two options. You can turn left on Old Chestnut Street, or you can cross it and continue on the narrower extension of the Graham Trail called the Boston Hill Loop. This one-mile loop ascends Boston Hill. At the top there is a clearing with spectacular 180-degree views from the northeast to southwest, including the skyline of Boston. If you take the full Boston Hill Loop, turn right when you return to Old Chestnut Street to continue this circuit.

Old Chestnut Street was one of Andover's main roads two hundred years ago. As you walk between its stone walls (something must love a wall, for these to have lasted so long), you will get a distinct impression of what it must have been like to travel from one place to another when horse power and feet were the only means of terrestrial locomotion. Think about bad weather and the darkness after early winter nightfall, and about how welcome a smoky, ale-fragrant inn must have been.

Old Chestnut Street leads to an electric company supply depot, recognizable by the abrupt visual intrusion of cable spools in a lot on your right. Just at the point where the lot begins, the Ward Trail veers sharply off to your left. Follow the trail for 0.8 mile to an intersection, where you should bear left. Another quarter-mile's walk will bring you back to the Holt Hill access road. Turn right here for the short walk down to the parking lot. (Note: As of this writing, the trails at the Ward Reservation are not thoroughly marked. It is advisable to hike with a map or, at least, with this guide. Future plans call for a scheme of letter identification at trail intersections, and a two-color outbound-inbound blazing system.)

There is one path that begins at the same side of Prospect Road as the parking lot and leads downhill. This is the Bog Trail, which takes you into the bog which borders Pine Hole Pond.

The Bog Trail starts at the southern end of the parking lot, to your left as you face the information board and map. The 1,100-foot trail ends at a 700-foot boardwalk that crosses the bog.

If a pond has no inlet or outlet — if, like Pine Hole Pond, it depends simply upon precipitation and spillage for replenishment and discharge — and if acid and soil conditions favor the growth of sphagnum moss around its banks, the formation of a bog may begin. Bogs develop as a shelf of humus, created by the death and decay of plants, spreads out from the banks of the pond. Colonies of living plants take hold on this shelf of organic matter, contributing in their turn to its thickening and expansion. A bog is not a static natural feature (in the long run, what is?) but an ongoing process of reclamation. The humus shelf, which in places may even quake and undulate above its uncertain basement of muck and water, will eventually cover the last open surface of the pond, and the final chapter in the bog's existence will involve the succession of dry-land plants above a layer of compacted peat. Plants that predominate in a pond-turned-bog such as the one we are visiting will include a specialized assortment of species such as leatherleaf, sheep laurel, and pitcher plants. Pitcher plants and other insectivorous species manage to survive in the nitrogen-deficient bog soils because of their ability to extract essential nitrogen from their prey.

A peculiarity of the bog surrounding Pine Hole Pond is the prevalence of black spruce. Although this conifer is a commonly recognized bog species, here it is growing at the southern extreme of its range, in an area where white cedars begin to take over as the predominant bog tree. This particular bog is an "island," with its own microclimate, where lower soil temperatures have no doubt contributed to the survival of this southern outpost of black spruce.

To learn more about bogs in general and the Ward Reservation's bog in particular, read the *Bog Nature Trail* guide, available for a small charge at the reservation or from the Trustees of Reservations at their Milton headquarters (address given above). The guide is coded to points along the boardwalk, and contains a good introductory explanation of bog ecology.

The Charles W. Ward Reservation, Prospect Road, Andover, Massachusetts is open from sunrise to sunset throughout the year.

10

LOWELL

A city walk that leads both to the origins of large-scale industrialism in America, and to the earliest social and visual influences on an important modern writer. A national park visitors' center helps provide orientation.

EVER SINCE *Country Walks Near Boston*, the first volume in this series, appeared in 1976, there has been a tradition of including in these books one chapter about a place that really isn't "country" by any stretch of the imagination, but still yields pleasures to the walker that equal in their way any that might be derived from observing the natural landscape. There is an urban landscape, too, textured and many-layered like those which lie far from city streets. In this walk we'll take a look around Lowell, not an old city by Massachusetts standards, but one which, like Boston, was the cradle of a revolution: a revolution not of muskets and drums and republican defiance, but of canals, turbines, spindles, and looms, of rackety brick factories announcing in a river of strong cotton cloth that the old, handspun America was passing.

There are mill towns, and there are mill towns. What makes Lowell unique is not only its standing as the first large-scale, planned manufacturing center (an honor challenged by Paterson, New Jersey, whose water-powered factory operations were conceived some thirty years before Lowell's, but which did not really get down to business until well after Lowell's wheels were turning), but also that Lowell has been made the site of a new National Historical Park which vividly commemorates the

industrial past and preserves many of the old mill buildings.

There is something else: Lowell was the birthplace and boyhood home of the novelist Jack Kerouac, who — despite his broader reputation as the chronicler of the Beat Generation — must also be remembered for the moving recollection of his days in the working-class quarters of this city set down in *The Town and the City, Visions of Gerard, Doctor Sax, Maggie Cassidy,* and *Vanity of Duluoz*. This walk around Lowell incorporates sites of industrial significance along the river and canals that brought them to life, and also passes by several of Kerouac's haunts and residences. The two are connected by more than mere physical proximity: it was the mills that brought French Canadians like the Kerouacs to Lowell (to this day there are *Quebecois* who think it is the capital of Massachusetts), and Jack Kerouac's was a factory-town childhood.

AUTOMOBILE: Take Interstate 93 north to Interstate 495 south; get off on the Lowell Connector and follow the signs first for downtown Lowell and then for Lowell National Historical Park. There is public parking along Dutton Street and in a municipal garage on Market Street, downtown.

PUBLIC TRANSPORTATION: Boston and Maine/MBTA commuter trains run from North Station, Boston, to the Thorndike Rail Terminal on Thorndike Street, Lowell. Walk north on Thorndike Street, crossing the Pawtucket Canal; turn right on Dutton Street and continue until you reach Market Street. Turn right here and look for the Visitor Center on your right.

There was a settlement — a small group of houses, nothing more — at Lowell long before the place got its present name or anyone thought of using the power of the swift Merrimack for manufacturing. In the eighteenth century it was called East Chelmsford. In 1792, a syndicate of Newburyport businessmen started work on the Pawtucket Canal, but they envisioned the

LOWELL

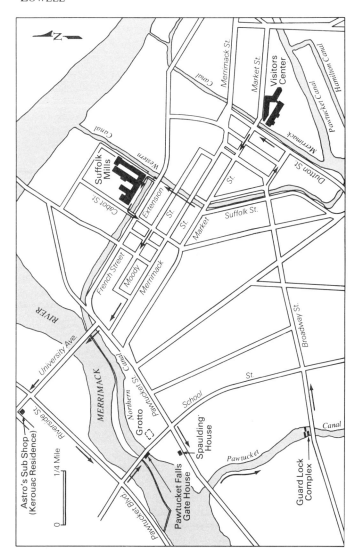

completed waterway not as a means of turning machinery but simply as a route around the Pawtucket Falls for shipments of lumber. The company they formed was the Proprietors of Locks and Canals on the Merrimack River, and it endures to this day as the holder of the canals in Lowell as well as several of the mills along their banks.

Lowell's modern history begins with the founding of the Boston Associates by Francis Cabot Lowell and several of his fellow Boston financiers. The group set up its first textile manufacturing operation, cloth from raw fiber, in Waltham, nearer to Boston. In 1821 they set out to choose a site for a vastly expanded, integrated facility. They settled upon East Chelmsford, where in the following year they established the Merrimack Manufacturing Company and began constructing mills and expanding the network of canals. The town was renamed Lowell, after Francis Cabot Lowell, who had died in 1817.

The success of the Lowell venture was virtually instantaneous, and continued through the building of new mills and canals, incorporation of Lowell as a city, and the importation of labor first from New England farms (the "Female Operatives" who broke ground for women factory workers) and later from among Canadian and European immigrants.

By the turn of the present century Lowell, like the other Merrimack River manufacturing cities of Lawrence, Massachusetts and Manchester, New Hampshire, was one of the great textile cities of the world, its streets echoing with the cacophony of power looms and the languages of a dozen nations. But the heyday was brief. The triple blows of labor unrest, depression, and migration of industry to the south made Lowell, by the time of Jack Kerouac's youth in the 1930s, a city whose best days seemed quite definitely past. At the outset of the 1970s things were even worse; Lowell had the highest unemployment rate in Massachusetts. But an economic reprieve arrived in the form of high-tech jobs — a northern extension of the Route-128 boom. And an immeasurable but equally important boost to civic pride came with designation of the downtown core area as Lowell

LOWELL

National Historical Park. Within the park, and in the Historic Preservation District that borders it, are restored mills, refurbished low-head hydroelectric generators, canal barge rides, guided interpretive tours, and a pair of brand-new open trolleys, duplicates of the type in use in Lowell circa 1900, which will run along the mile of track that links the downtown mills with the canal-barge boarding area.

Information on all park programs and attractions is available at the Visitors' Center, 245 Market Street. This 1828 building, which originally belonged to the Lowell Manufacturing Company, houses exhibits explaining the roles of labor and capital in building Lowell, a bookstore, and an eighteen-projector slide show on the city and its history that is highly recommended. This is also the point at which the walk outlined here begins. (For other walks and guided tour schedules, consult the rangers at the Visitors' Center, 617-459-1000.)

THE WALK: Turn left as you leave the Visitors' Center courtyard, and follow Market Street across the Merrimack Canal. The route takes you through what is still a predominately Greek neighborhood; Greeks began arriving in Lowell in the late 1890s and soon established one of the strongest ethnic presences in the city. Continue on Market Street until you cross the Western Canal, and turn right on Suffolk Street. Follow Suffolk, alongside the canal, until you pass the French Street Extension, cross the Northern Canal, and stand at the corner of the vast red-brick expanse of the Suffolk Mills. This is where the trolley route terminates and visitors may board canal barges in summer.

The Suffolk Manufacturing Company was organized in 1830 by the Lawrence Brothers, who obtained this site, along with two others in Lowell, for textile mills. Construction of this mill complex began in late 1830 or early 1831 and paralleled completion of work on the Western Canal, from which it was to derive power. As with most Lowell mill buildings of the time,

the general contractor was the Proprietors of Locks and Canals (PL&C). Records of the era show that the PL&C invoiced the Suffolk Manufacturing Company for 1,480,366 bricks, 268 tons of stone, 13,941 pounds of forged iron, and 903,000 board feet of lumber, all used in construction of the original structure, at a total price of just under $68,000.

The mill was substantially expanded in 1844, and in 1862 the three buildings on the site were consolidated and enlarged. The year 1880 saw even more expansion, and by 1900 the mill stood essentially as we see it now. It was purchased by the Nashua Manufacturing Company in 1926, and closed ten years later. Only parts of the complex remained in use thereafter; in 1950 the Wannalancit Textile Company took over and kept up operations until 1981. When this firm shut down its looms, Lowell's long history of producing cloth from natural fibers came to an end.

Today, the Suffolk Mill houses Park exhibits of textile and water power machinery which are open daily in summer and to tours during the rest of the year. Two of the hydroelectric turbines at the site are scheduled to return to operation during the mid-1980s.

Walk along the Northern Canal to Cabot Street. Turn left on Cabot, crossing the canal (built in 1847), and proceed one block to Moody Street; then turn right on Moody.

You are now in what was once called "Little Canada," a place where there are still many French names on the mailboxes and where the Church of St. Jean Baptiste is the most imposing physical and spiritual presence. You will pass the rear of this church on your left as you walk along Moody Street. Jack Kerouac's funeral mass was said there in 1969. When Kerouac lived in Lowell, Moody Street extended all the way across the Merrimack via the Moody Street Bridge, a structure that looms large in books like *Doctor Sax*. (*Sax* contains a chapter titled "The Night the Man With the Watermelon Died," in which

Kerouac describes walking across the bridge with his mother and seeing a man carrying a watermelon drop dead on the planks — "his eyes had turned glassy on the milky waters of the night in their hollow roar cold rock.") At the corner of Moody and Pawtucket Streets, where the new hospital buildings now cut Moody off from the river, stood St. Joseph's School, where Kerouac learned English as a first-grader.

Turn left at the end of Moody Street (look back here for a good view of the mills along the river) and walk one block to Merrimack Street. Turn right and follow Merrimack to its end at Pawtucket Street, then right again and left to cross the University Avenue Bridge. To your right, on the near shore, is the site of a new hydroelectric project.

On the opposite shore is the old French Canadian neighborhood of Pawtucketville. Here are the buildings of the University of Lowell, formed several years ago when Lowell State College merged with the Textile Institute. At 118 University Avenue (left side) is Astro's Sub Shop, occupying the ground floor of a four-story wooden tenement where the Kerouac family lived while Jack was a teenager. Their apartment was at the upper right on the top floor, as you face the building; Jack's room was at the rear.

Backtrack along University Avenue for one block until you reach Riverside Street; then turn right (Riverside becomes Pawtucket Boulevard along here) and continue until you reach the School Street Bridge. Cross the bridge, looking to the right to see the Pawtucket Falls which suggested the idea of water-powered mills to the early entrepreneurs.

As you reach the opposite side of the School Street Bridge, two structures — one dramatically religious, the other simple and utilitarian — appear on the left and right. At left, on the grounds behind the Franco-American School, is the Grotto and

Lowell

Stations of the Cross built by the Oblate Fathers in 1911. Reminiscent of the fantastic shrines of Quebec, the Grotto and its vivid crucifixion scene alternately aroused feelings of piety and spookiness in young Kerouac: "... the Cross itself ... with its Poor Burden the Son of Man all skewered across it in his Agony and Fright — undoubtedly this statue moved in the night ..." And it was through the shadows of the Grotto that Doctor Sax, a caped, slouch-hatted phantom, half menace and half protector, moved silently in the Merrimack night of the boy's imagination.

The low brick building on the right side of the bridge is the Pawtucket Falls Gatehouse. This was the largest of the gatehouses on the Lowell canal system; it houses ten working gates, along with a functioning belt and pulley system, and a nonfunctioning eleventh gate that formerly let in the water that activated the other ten. Today the gates are activated electrically, and the water they admit still turns turbines that create hydroelectric power. In summer, costumed interpreters explain how the gatehouses work.

Continue on School Street to Pawtucket Street and turn right, passing the 1760 Spalding House (right), which predated the beginning of Lowell's industrial era by over sixty years. Pawtucket Street soon crosses the Pawtucket Canal; turn left here and follow the pathway along the right side of the canal.

Up ahead on your right is a large brick building with blue awnings, originally the Pilling Shoe Company factory and one of the first of the old Lowell mills to be restored — in this case, as housing for the elderly. Opposite the Pilling Building and standing astride the canal are the three buildings that constitute the Guard Lock complex. The tan-colored building, fully restored, was erected over the massive wooden Francis Gate, installed in 1850 for flood-control. It was originally called "Francis' Folly" (after its builder, hydraulic engineer James B.

LOWELL

Francis) and thought unnecessary, but as soon as 1852 and again in 1936 it proved its worth by acting as a relief valve for the rampaging Merrimack. (The 1936 flood is impressionistically documented in *Doctor Sax*; Kerouac was fourteen when it happened.)

The other two buildings straddling the canal are the circa 1820s sluice gatehouse (part wooden, part brick) which housed the gates that regulated water for power purposes; and the older, near-derelict wooden structure built over the lock chamber that kept river water from surging in when the canal was first used for transportation — the so-called "Guard Lock." As of this writing, both of these buildings are scheduled for renovation.

Broadway crosses the Pawtucket Canal just after the Guard Lock complex. Turn left here and head back downtown, bearing right after you cross the Western Canal and turning left on Dutton Street. After one block, turn right on Market Street and cross the Merrimack Canal, and the Visitors' Center will be on your right.

Contact Lowell National Historical Park, 169 Merrimack Street, Lowell, MA 01852 (617-459-1000), for further information on the city's mills and historic sites, and for schedules of tours and events.

The resting place of Jean Louis Lebris de Kerouac is in Edson Cemetery, off Gorham Street 2 miles south of the city center.

11

BROADMOOR WILDLIFE SANCTUARY

Walking and ski touring — 9 miles of trails lead through historic grown-over farmland on the banks of the Charles River, and past the site of one of the area's early lumber and grain milling ventures.

To MANY BOSTONIANS, the Charles River is a tidal estuary that starts at Harvard College and ends at the Museum of Science. It's pretty to look at from the Esplanade, they will tell you, and fun to sail on, but you wouldn't want to fall in. They tend to forget that the Charles meanders for quite some distance before it even reaches Boston and Cambridge, and that for most of the way it is a narrower, cleaner river of vastly different character. A visit to Massachusetts Audubon's Broadmoor Wildlife Sanctuary, in South Natick and Sherborn, affords a look at that other Charles River, and at the farmland and small-time industrial activities that it once nurtured.

Broadmoor is one of Mass. Audubon's newer sanctuaries. The property of 577 acres, which is bordered on the east by the Charles, was assembled from separate gifts of land in 1962, 1968, and 1972, and the Society's purchase of a 23-acre farm in 1973. But the history of this land's use and development goes back a good deal farther, to a time in the 1600s when all was the recognized property of the local Natick Indians.

Before 1620, of course, all of Massachusetts belonged to the Indians. The arrival of the colonists, with their European ideas of land ownership and grants, deeds, compacts, and divisions, changed all that and made the natives petitioners for their own

collective patrimony. In 1651, the Massachusetts General Court set aside 6,000 acres from the Dedham Grant for the Natick Indians, who for most of the remainder of the century were the only ones allowed residence in their town. They even handled their own civic and religious affairs (having been made good Congregationalists through the offices of men like the Reverend John Eliot, whom we met when we visited Brook Farm's Pulpit Rock in Chapter 3) and in general kept charge of affairs on what must have been one of the first "reservations" in North America.

The Naticks did need some European technological assistance, though, in the form of a gristmill. They had been bringing their grain to Medfield and Watertown for grinding — not an inconsiderable trip by footpath in those days — and petitioned the General Court to let Thomas Sawin, a Sherborn carpenter, own land and set up a mill within their property. The Court acceded, and in 1692 Sawin relocated in Natick.

The site of the mill Sawin built for his clientele of Indians and colonists was along what is now called Indian Brook, which flows from Little Pond and the Charles River through the heart of the Broadmoor Sanctuary. The brook was dammed and a mill pond created; eventually, a sawmill stood there as well. The property stayed in the Sawin family until 1858, when it was purchased by John Morse. Morse and his son continued to run the mills into the 1900s; the sawmill was destroyed by fire in 1918 and the gristmill was torn down by a new owner, Carl Stillman, when he took possession of the property in the 1920s. Stillman's heirs donated the mill pond and surrounding property to Audubon in 1968.

More than the mill pond has changed over the past three hundred years at Broadmoor. As we have seen with so many of the old farmlands of eastern Massachusetts, open fields have given way to the successional growth of oak and white pine; what clear meadows remain are kept so through efforts of the sanctuary management. Near the Charles, the woods are especially thick; overhanging branches give the banks of the muddy river a decidedly Amazonian appearance.

BROADMOOR WILDLIFE SANCTUARY

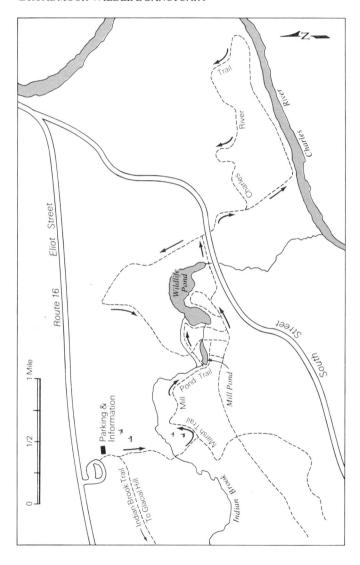

101

AUTOMOBILE: From Boston, take either Route 9 or the Massachusetts Turnpike west to Route 16. Take Route 16 south into Natick, where it becomes Eliot Street. The entrance to the sanctuary is on your left, 1.8 miles west of South Natick Center.

THE WALK: There are 9 miles of mostly well-marked trails at Broadmoor, originating at the parking area and information center. The Indian Brook Trail leads off to the right, joining with the Glacial Hill Trail to reach (3 miles) the top of a 200-foot drumlin which is the highest point within the sanctuary. The trail that leads off to the left behind the visitors' center offers the most varied sampling of the Broadmoor's terrain and historical associations. Follow the trail across Indian Brook to its juncture with the Mill Pond/Marsh Trail. Turn left and follow this trail to the old Mill Pond. The trail will take you through a white pine plantation on the edge of a marsh.

At the head of the pond a small footbridge takes you across the old impoundment. Nothing remains of the old mill buildings today, although the sawmill site is marked by several small pools and the stone foundations of Thomas Sawin's original gristmill are visible just ahead, between the Mill Pond and the larger Wildlife Pond. Two millstones are still at the site. The Wildlife Pond is a recent addition, the result of rebuilding an old farm dam in 1971. Ducks, geese, painted turtles, and river otters all have been attracted to the new pond.

Follow the trail that skirts the banks of the Wildlife Pond, bearing first right and then left, until you are walking parallel to South Street. At a point just a few hundred yards past the pond outlet, the trail crosses South Street and becomes the Charles River Trail. Follow the trail uphill to a fork; you may head in either direction (the trail is a continuous loop) but bearing to the right will get you to the river bank sooner.

The slopes above the river are forested in the oaks and white pines typical of more seasoned upland forest in this latitude; less than a hundred years ago, this land would most likely have been pasture. The walk towards and along the river bank is a descent into a darker, damper world, where tupelo and red maple predominate. During spring and rainy seasons, you will likely find the riverbank portion of the trail mucky and difficult if you are not wearing rubber boots.

The Charles, at this early stage in its descent to the sea (it still has to flow past or through Wellesley, Needham, Dover, Dedham, West Roxbury, Newton, Weston, Waltham and Watertown before reaching tidewater at Cambridge and downtown Boston), is a river that still exhibits many of the characteristics of a healthy coastal lowland stream, with a number of its original fish and benthic (bottom-dwelling) invertebrate species still in evidence. As you can see from the downstream municipal litany above, it is still minus a good deal of pollution at this point. This is the preindustrial Charles, looking no doubt much the way it did before the fields at Broadmoor were first cleared.

Make the Charles River Trail loop and head back to the visitors' center and parking area the way you came. One alternative along the way is to continue straight, rather than turning left, immediately after crossing South Street. This spur route will take you into higher ground farther from the Wildlife Pond, but will rejoin the main Mill Pond/Marsh Trail at the Mill Pond. Remember the system of blazes: blue dots mean that you are headed away from the parking area, yellow dots take you back, and white dots mark connector trails.

The visitors' center at Broadmoor is itself one of the attractions. In 1983, Mass. Audubon completed conversion of this old barn to a state-of-the-art passive solar building, complete with superinsulation (R28 walls, R40 ceiling, R6 floor slab),

Broadmoor Wildlife Sanctuary

sunspace with both rock bed and water tube thermal storage, natural ventilation and cooling, woodstove, and a composting toilet that saves over 100,000 gallons of water each year. Complete information on the building, now called the Broadmoor Nature Center, is available at the front desk. Also stop to see the natural history exhibits and to ask about special programs such as field courses, guided tours, and bird walks. "Birds and Breakfast Day," held each May, is an annual highlight.

Broadmoor Wildlife Sanctuary, 280 Eliot Street, Natick, MA 01760, is open daily except Mondays throughout the year from dawn to dusk. A modest admission fee is charged visitors who are not members of the Massachusetts Audubon Society.

12

PLUM ISLAND/
PARKER RIVER WILDLIFE REFUGE

Walking — one of the largest and best-preserved barrier beaches on the North Atlantic coast. Enjoy walks through or along primary and secondary dunes, salt and freshwater marshes, and scrub forest; also some of the finest coastal birding in the country. Nearby is Old Town Hill, where a short walk pays off in splendid views.

PLUM ISLAND is northern Essex County's front line of defense against the Atlantic. If you walk down Water Street in Newburyport, you will come upon something called the "seawall," but that isn't the sea on the other side; it's only the Joppa Flats, a distention of the outlet of the Merrimack River that can scarcely float a dory at high tide. At low tide you can walk along the outside of the Water Street seawall. You don't reach open ocean until you cross Plum Island.

Long before it started throwing shuttles in the textile mills of Manchester and Lowell or floating Newburyport clippers, the Merrimack River assisted the Wisconsin ice sheet in forming the barrier beach that we call Plum Island. In the days of the glacier, some 12,000 years ago, the coast of Massachusetts was out somewhere near Georges Bank. As the ice receded, there began a 5,000-year contest between the sea, newly flooded with meltwater, and the land, rebounding from the crushing weight of the glacier, to determine the new shoreline. Roughly 3,500 years ago, these elemental forces arrived at a compromise. Then the

river and the sea began working on the finishing touch, the barrier beach.

East of what is now Ipswich and Rowley, the retreating glacier had left behind drumlins, stubborn mounds of boulders bound with clay. Four of these are large enough to have names: Grape Island, Bar Head, Stage Island, and Cross Farm Hill. The last three were destined to anchor Plum Island. The Merrimack brought silt to the Atlantic, and as the currents carried it southward toward Cape Ann, the drumlins held it fast. Like the grains around which a pearl coalesces in the belly of an oyster, they grew larger. Finally, they joined together to become the southern bastion of Plum Island.

The Merrimack silt continued to pile northward, back towards the river's mouth. Meanwhile, the tides kept drawing upon the enormous moraine deposits that lie offshore, adding these to the new formation. Quartz, feldspar, and clay, bulldozed by the glacier from as far away as Nova Scotia and pounded by the ocean into sand, were alternately piled against the barrier, as they are still, and taken away — in what very nearly amounts to a closed system — by the waves.

The salt marsh followed. Protected by Plum Island from the brunt of the Atlantic, the lands around Broad Sound and the Parker River burgeoned with life. The island itself was no less fecund. From the bright, austere primary dunes to the brackish fens that face the mainland, sand- and salt-hardy species of plants and animals thrived. The Agawam Indians called this place "heaven." They spent many summers here; it suited their predilection for the easy life. There are still shell middens in the back dunes.

AUTOMOBILE: From Boston, take Route 1 north to Interstate 95 and continue north to Route 113. Take the exit for Newburyport. Drive 3 miles into town. If you wish to see Newburyport, turn left at Green Street and park downtown, heading out later to Plum Island via Merrimack Street (along the river) and the Plum Island Turnpike. To bypass Newbury-

Plum Island

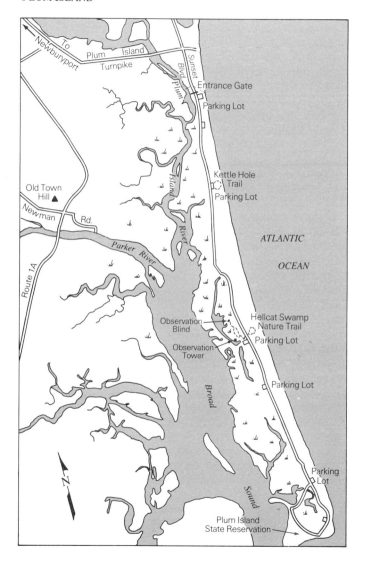

port Center, stay on High Street (Route 113 feeds into High Street, which then becomes Route 1A) until you reach Newbury Green. Bear left at the fork by the Green and turn left at the traffic light. Follow Rolfe's Lane to the Plum Island Turnpike and turn right.

After crossing the bridge to the Island, take the first right to reach the refuge gate.

It was early in the seventeenth century that Englishmen first saw Plum Island. According to their earliest reports, they found a dense climax forest of white pine, which meant ships' masts and lumber. After it was cleared, cattle were put to pasture here. This not only kept the forest from recovering but also stripped the grasses from the soil. By the middle of the eighteenth century, nearly all of the island's vegetation had been lost to grazing. When Henry Thoreau came in 1839, he found that Plum Island made for "a grand and dreary walk."

During the century that followed, a cessation of grazing allowed the vegetation to recoup, although the great forests have never come back. In 1942, the U.S. Fish and Wildlife Service established the Parker River National Wildlife Refuge, which comprises 4,650 acres of the southern three-quarters of Plum Island and its adjacent marshland. At the time, the northern quarter of the island was occupied by only two hundred year-round residents and a scattering of summer visitors.

In strict legal terms there is no town called "Plum Island." The community on the northern end of the island now numbers 1,800 permanent inhabitants, plus the summer colony, but it is still divided between Newburyport and Newbury. Many of the year-rounders are fishermen, and it was undoubtedly their independence and contentiousness as much as the peculiar geography of the place that caused talk about secession a few years ago. But the property taxes still go to the mainland, and it is from mainland town halls that services are deployed.

If you head out from Newburyport on the Plum Island Turnpike, you will skirt the southern margins of the Joppa Flats, cross the Plum Island River, and touch land again at a point just a half-mile north of the refuge gates. If you turn right here, you will see very little of the island's inhabited portion before entering the refuge. But if you go up to the next intersection and turn left you will be on Plum Island's main drag. Northern Boulevard is lined with houses that bring to mind sand-strewn linoleum floors and clamshell ashtrays. There are fried clam joints with names like "Surfcaster's Galley," a liquor store, a church, and shops selling the grotesque little sea worms that flounder and pollack prefer. The boulevard and its grandly numbered side alleys ("58th Street," "76th Street") are mostly residential. Lately, cottage winterizations have been outstripping new construction ten to one. More and more people seem to like living here all year, and they make whatever arrangements are necessary to do so.

THE WALK: There is a series of parking lots along the single access road within the Parker River Wildlife Refuge. The largest is just beyond the entrance; the remainder can accommodate a dozen or so cars each, with connecting walkways to the beach. The number and location of these parking areas may well change over the next few years as new management plans are implemented at the refuge. One thing, however, will not change: visitors are strongly discouraged from leaving the walkways between the road and the beach because the dunes and their vegetation are fragile.

To view a good cross-section of the refuge's scenery and ecosystems — from the salt marsh and thicketed swamp along the inland side, to the secondary dune environment on the ocean side of the road — take the Hellcat Swamp Trail, which has parking on the right several miles beyond the entrance gate. There are also an observation tower and birding blind adjacent to this route.

Near the observation tower at the beginning of Hellcat Swamp Trail is an impoundment built thirty years ago to divide

fresh water from the salt marsh along Broad Sound. With this bit of earthwork the Fish and Wildlife Service has made a curious ecological club sandwich; to the east there are the woods and dunes of Plum Island proper; then the elongated pools of fresh water and their accompanying marshes; next there is the dike; and finally salt water and salt marsh. Within a few yards of each other live creatures, plant and animal, that would die if they could travel back and forth. One of these is a newcomer to Plum Island, the beaver.

How the beavers got there is a good question. Salt water kills them; people have found carcasses of beavers that died trying to make the crossing. One guess is that the beavers living on the island today made it across Ipswich Sound after a heavy thunderstorm, when there was a good layer of fresh water on top of the salt. Now that the beavers are there, they seem to be doing well. The Fish and Wildlife Service will have to decide how many will be allowed to stay; beavers are tough on aspen trees. One family of beavers may prove to be enough on this land. If there get to be too many, rangers may have to live-trap them and move them out.

To the south of the tower is a goose-browse field, one of several on the island. These marshes are very much a goose neighborhood. The refuge was founded primarily as a haven for migratory waterfowl, and the Canada Goose is its main beneficiary. About eighty-eight acres are planted in grasses, mostly fescue, thistle, and vetch, and are mowed by Fish and Wildlife Service personnel each year after nesting season. There is now a resident year-round population of about a hundred geese, mostly descended from pairs brought here in the 1950s and raised in pens. The geese like Plum Island. They benefit from the browse fields, but they would probably stay here even if no planting was done.

As you make your way along the Hellcat Swamp Trail towards the sea, keep in mind that one of the things that makes Plum Island so special is that you can traverse five different ecosystems here in a short space of time. There are both salt and freshwater marshes, back dunes, primary dunes, and the sea beach. On the whole, of course, the flora, the plant cover is more varied. Virginia creeper mingles with poison ivy, which is tremendously abundant here. Cherry — several species — and arrowwood rise in thickets everywhere. There is pitch pine, an early successional species, and Japanese black pine, stands of which were planted by the Fish and Wildlife Service. Like the plants, the animals on Plum Island include familiar inland species; there are rabbits, woodchucks, foxes, garter snakes, mice. The eastern long-tailed jumping mouse lives here. A startled jumping mouse, or even one simply going about his business, can leap six feet.

The snakes, mice, and rabbits keep the raptors busy; marsh hawks, red-tailed hawks, and kestrels are common. At Plum Island, though, raptors aren't the half of it. Waterfowl, shorebirds, assorted confusing warblers, and a Peterson's potpourri of both regulars and accidentals bring birders in every season. Some years ago, all the talk was of Ross's gull. In 1981, a white pelican turned up.

Eventually, the back dunes give way to the primary dunes. Along the intermediate zone between them (you may or may not see any from the trail) are swales, hollows protected from the scouring winds and fed by sea water that has lost its salinity through underground percolation. A few feet, one way or the other, can make the difference for a swale. If they get a little bit of extra protection from the wind, they can support intensive vegetation. Deer will visit, birds will nest, a woodchuck might live along the edge. Given enough ground water, a swale might develop into a cranberry bog. Then there will be sundew, pitcher plants, and other bog species.

When you reach the primary dunes — the front rank — you are among the most dynamic of Plum Island's shifting sandhills. These dunes are where the energy of the sea is absorbed. A handful of plants survive here, but they make all the difference: beach grass — its subsurface rhizomes racing every which way — beach pea, false heather, and dusty miller, husbanding mois-

ture within its furry leaves. They secure the dunes from above, as the drumlins anchor the island from below. They are why the people who keep the refuge do not want you wandering off the trails.

To arrive at the open ocean is to have finished a walk backward through time. "Sand," says Plum Island naturalist Michael Hoel, "is one of the greatest reductions of nature. After millions of years of washing and blowing around, of being ground and polished, what you get are pieces of quartz or granite that are nearly irreducible. They represent the hardest part of whatever material they descended from. The sand on Plum Island could be a billion years old."

The finest sand is nearest the water. It is the floor, the foundation of the world that lives between high and low tide. The grains here never touch; each is surrounded by its own globule of water, within which live dynoflagellates and other microorganisms. The bacteria that feed these microorganisms are the first course of a vertically integrated banquet that progresses to the decks of trawlers and the bellies of great whales.

At the mammalian end of the evolutionary spectrum on Plum Island are not only jumping mice, beavers, and human beings, but also white-tailed deer. There are about twenty deer on the island in an average year, but their numbers increase during hunting season, when deer wade across the marshes from the mainland. They know what "refuge" means. Even so, they are not so bold as to assure frequent sightings. You may come upon a deer crossing the road during the early morning or evening hours when traffic is light; more likely you will not. In the latter case, it's something to look forward to on your next visit, or the next after that.

Parker River National Wildlife Refuge is open every day of the year from dawn to dusk. Admission and parking are free. If you have a night fishing permit — and you can get one only if you apply while in possession of surf-casting tackle — you can stay on the beach all night, providing everyone in your party is fishing.

Plum Island

In summer, make sure you arrive at the refuge by 8 A.M. or 9 A.M., since no cars or pedestrians are allowed to enter after the parking lots have filled. When that happens, you'll usually have to wait until about 3 P.M. to gain admission.

A pleasant side trip from Plum Island or Newburyport takes you to Old Town Hill, Newbury, managed by the Massachusetts Trustees of Public Reservations. Old Town Hill occupies the highest ground in Newbury, and from the clearings atop its forested slopes you can see New Hampshire and Maine to the north (along with the Isles of Shoals, on clear days), Plum Island and the Atlantic to the east, and the Rowley marshes, Ipswich, and Cape Ann to the south. The walk uphill is moderately steep but only several hundred yards long, with an optional longer trail back to the road.

To get to Old Town Hill from Newburyport, follow High Street to Newbury Green, bear right at the fork, and follow Green Street as far as it goes (about a mile). Turn right at Hay Street, then left on Newman Road. Cross the marshes and go over the hill; the reservation is just on your left before you reach Newbury Lower Green and Route 1A. There is limited parking along the road.

13

HOG ISLAND

A combination canoe trip and walk, with the destination the least known, least accessible, and perhaps most beautiful part of the vast Crane Reservation in Ipswich and Essex. Visit a colonial homestead and walk to the top of a reforested drumlin for commanding views of the salt marshes, estuaries, and barrier beaches north of Cape Ann.

SEARCH YOUR ATLAS in vain for a more prosaic place name than Hog Island; then search the coast of New England for anything more beautiful. Hog Island is a drumlin anchored in Essex Bay near where the Essex and Castle Neck rivers enter the bay, and protected from the open ocean by the arching promontory of Castle Neck. That said, we may as well add that St. Peter's Basilica is a large church in Rome, or that Herman Melville was an ex-seaman who wrote books. Simple recitation of locus and topography does little justice to Hog Island, and whatever we can muster in the way of prose and photography cannot do much more. To get the effect you'll just have to make the trip — and if it seems somewhat more complicated than is usual for these exurban outings, that is so much the more appropriate. This is less of a country walk than an expedition, by water and land, and the rewards are worth the effort.

Hog Island, with its surrounding marshes and smaller islands, comprises the Cornelius and Mine S. Crane Wildlife Refuge. It is the property of the Trustees of Reservations, who also own and manage the adjacent mainland Richard T. Crane Memorial Reservation. The island's serenity and ecological well-being are

MORE COUNTRY WALKS

protected by strict limitations on visitors, outlined at the end of this chapter. Briefly, these rules restrict visits to weekends and holidays in summer and early fall, with weekday trips allowed for members of the Friends of Hog Island.

There is no public boat access to Hog Island. While motorized approaches in small craft are feasible and permitted, we recommend that the trip from the mainland be made by canoe. This is in keeping not only with the spirit of this book, but with the character of the place. Anyway, a slow approach is best: let this brooding drumlin grow slowly on the near horizon, as you paddle into tidewater between the frayed and marshy banks of the Essex River.

BY AUTOMOBILE AND CANOE: Take Route 128 north to Route 133; follow 133 north to Essex. Just beyond Woodman's restaurant (which credits itself with the invention of the fried clam) there is a parking area on the left, adjacent to a small roadside park — look for the flagpole. You may park here after using the launching area opposite.

It is important to time your launch so that you will reach Hog Island within four hours on either side of high tide — consult tables for Ipswich and Essex bays. Barring headwinds, the trip from the Route 133 launch area should take a little more than one hour, closer to two if the tide is not in your favor. If you approach Hog Island in too low a tide, you will find the channels around the Great Bank (see map) too shallow to float a canoe. So, unless you want to hop out, shoulder the painter, and imitate Humphrey Bogart in The African Queen *(minus the leeches), watch the tides.*

Once you are out in the main channel of the Essex, Hog Island will loom unmistakeably ahead — just paddle straight for the heavily wooded, gently sloping hill. You will be able to make out the roof and chimneys of the Crane Mansion on Castle Hill, to your left; on the right, as you near Hog Island, you will see the Choate House and the island's two other buildings. Keep these buildings on your left as you bear right

HOG ISLAND

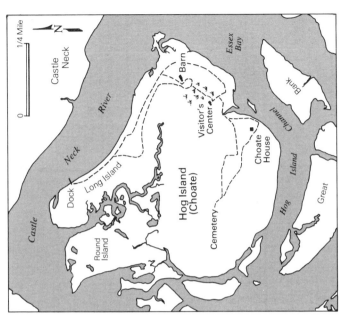

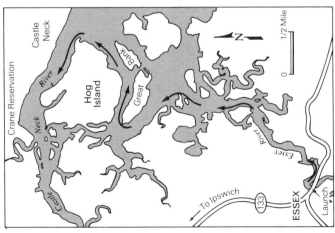

MORE COUNTRY WALKS

around the island, then left around its easternmost point, with the dunes of Castle Neck immediately ahead. The dock will be prominent on your left, as you approach the mouth of the Castle Neck River. Dock here and register with the first staff member you encounter.

THE WALK: The dock is actually on Long Island, a low, narrow finger of land connected to Hog Island by the salt marsh surrounding Lee's Creek and by a ridge at its eastern extreme, which remains passable at high tide. Turn left after docking; Castle Neck will be across the channel to your left, while directly behind you, beyond the Castle Neck River in neighboring Ipswich, rises Castle Hill and the great Georgian mansion built in 1926 by Richard T. Crane, Jr.

A look over our shoulders at the Crane Mansion reminds us of the legacy that has preserved Hog Island for us to this day. Chicago plumbing magnate Richard Crane bought Ipswich's Castle Hill Farm in 1910, as the first in a series of acquisitions which eventually left him in possession of some 3,500 coastal acres. He saw to it that the hill became worthy of its name by building upon it an elaborate Italianate villa. This was replaced, after only fifteen years, by the "Great House," with forty-nine rooms, which was bequeathed, along with much of the surrounding acreage, to the Trustees of Reservations by Crane's widow in 1949.

Crane had bought Hog Island in 1919. It remained in the family throughout the lifetime of his son, Cornelius Crane, who died in 1962; twelve years later the latter's widow, Mine Sawaraha Crane, made the island part of a further 700-acre bequest to the Trustees. We will see more of what the Crane family stewardship has meant for Hog Island as we continue a walk along its shores and into its elevated, wooded interior.

Follow the gravel road to where it forks. The low road will take you along the beach; the high road to the right continues

Hog Island

along a gentle ridge offering spacious views of the wooded slopes of Hog Island and the foreground marshes.

It is not unlikely that this upland walk will afford your first look at some of Hog Island's resident deer. There are, at last count, over seventy deer that spend the winter on the island, but their population is diminishing somewhat with summer migrations to the mainland. Deer thrive here because the forest offers protection in winter, because there are sufficient browse and grazing fields, and because the closest thing they encounter to predation is limited, special-season hunting on the mainland and nearby smaller islands, intended to control population and prevent attrition due to starvation and disease. There is never any hunting on Hog Island itself. The result is a colony of individuals which, while still innately wary, will venture a lot closer to humans than their mainland counterparts.

The heavy stand of spruce on Hog Island has not grown since time immemorial. When the colonists first encountered the northern coast of Massachusetts, there was dense evergreen cover throughout the area — on Hog Island as well as on larger Plum Island to the north. But three centuries of farming, grazing, and shipbuilding thoroughly denuded the coast, so that when Richard Crane took possession of his little fiefdom it presented a far different appearance than it does today. Crane had his estate superintendant, Robert Cameron, plant 100,000 trees on the island. These have since grown to maturity, and the forest is now being managed by the Trustees to assure its perpetuation. Of course, wilderness forests of many thousands of acres survive without management; but if a relatively small, monocultural stand like this is going to regenerate without fire, selective thinning and encouragement both of new spruce seedlings and of more diverse understory plants must continue.

The high road from the dock soon reaches the barn, and just beyond, it rejoins the beach path and continues across the marsh to Hog Island proper.

Hog Island

The barn on Hog Island was built about 1785. It was restored by Cornelius Crane; more recently, the Trustees have taken care of necessary reshingling and painting on this fine example of eighteenth-century utilitarian architecture. The barn overlooks a narrow salt marsh that separates Long Island from Hog; there are two routes to the white house opposite. Unless the tide is completely at ebb, take the drier outside path. The bridge which made the inside route passable at all times went out with the ice many years ago. This wasn't the only span to have fared poorly around here — somehow, Hog Island is not meant to be securely linked to its neighbors or to the mainland. In 1886, a bridge to Dean Island was built, but it was destroyed in the great storm of 1898. After that, foot, horse, and wagon traffic followed a gravel-stiffened route down the bed of Hardy's Creek to the island, but disuse made even this low-tide-only option impassable after the 1920s. In his book *Boston's Gold Coast*, Joseph Garland tells of a pre-Crane era summer resident who traveled back and forth by means of a wheelbarrow and a canoe, the state of the tides determining which conveyance was carried in which.

The white house up ahead was built by the Cranes in the 1940s. Today, it serves as a residence for the wintertime caretaker and as a nature center in which visitors may view photographs and artifacts depicting the island's history, as well as mounted specimens of some of the 202 bird species that have been recorded within the Crane Refuge.

The oldest of Hog Island's three buildings stands on a grassy hillside just ahead, and may be reached by following the gravel road from the white house. This is the ancestral residence of the Choate family, who bought the island in the late 1600s. The house, which is open to visitors in summer, was built about 1725 and inhabited until 1913. Rufus Choate, who succeeded to Daniel Webster's Senate seat in 1841 and was known as the greatest trial lawyer of his day, was born here in 1799.

The Choates' ownership of this land, which they farmed and used for grazing sheep for the better part of two centuries, accounts for its alternate name of Choate Island. The appellation

Hog Island is due, according to varying stories, to its proximity to "Hogtown," an old name for a part of Ipswich; the profile of the island; or its sometime use as a pasture for swine.

The Cranes did not use this house, although Richard Crane restored it in the early 1920s. By 1977, the Trustees were faced with the task of reversing major deterioration of the old structure and the job they have done appears sound. The huge kitchen hearth, graceful Rumford fireplaces, and built-in hearthside cupboards all mark this as an example of the early New England ideal: a house built around a massive chimney, rather than a chimney simply rising from a house.

Follow the gravel road which leads uphill at the rear of the Choate House. It skirts the forest at the edge of the meadow and rises to the 177-foot crest of Hog Island, where there is an opening, with views to the north, and the Crane burial place. Stay on the road; entering the forest is discouraged.

The small, chain-encircled burial plot at the top of the hill is the resting place of Cornelius Crane, who along with his wife Mine was the last private owner of Hog Island. Look north, through the opening in the forest, to see the drumlins and marshes surrounding the mouth of the Ipswich River and Plum Island Sound, and the southern tip of Plum Island itself. Here, as well as anywhere on the island, you will understand why the diplomat Joseph Hodges Choate, on visiting his family's ancesttral home in 1898, remarked, "I would rather be governor of Hog Island than all of Massachusetts."

Return to the dock the way you came, following the gravel road past the two houses and barn. The canoe route back to Route 133 is likewise a reverse of the outbound passage, although with the increased likelihood of paddling up a short blind channel or two as you approach the landing. Again, be sure to time your departure according to the tides — a more

Hog Island

crucial factor in the immediate vicinity of the island than in the river approach to Route 133.

The Cornelius and Mine S. Crane Wildlife Refuge (Hog Island), property of the Trustees of Reservations, is open to the general public between 9:30 A.M. and 3:00 P.M. on weekends and holidays between Memorial Day and Columbus Day. Members of the Trustees and of the Friends of Hog Island are admitted on weekdays during that season. The designated boat landing must be used. Upon landing, register with a staff member for authorization to take an unguided tour. The fee is $2.00 for adults, $1.00 for children 6 to 14 (free to members of above organizations). Guided tours may be arranged in advance by calling 356-3458 between 5:30 and 6:30 on weekdays; the fee is $3.00 and the group limit is 25. For a complete copy of the refuge regulations and information on joining the Friends of Hog Island, contact the Trustees of Reservations, 224 Adams Street, Milton, MA 02186.

14

WINNEKENNI PARK

Walking and ski touring — a visit to the land John Greenleaf Whittier loved, with a 3-mile lakeside trail and other paths within a Haverhill city park that contains a restored stone "castle." Nearby are Whittier's Haverhill birthplace and, in Amesbury, his lifelong home.

NOW WE ARE IN Whittier country. The great "fireside poet" of the nineteenth century, who always felt most at home in the rural and small-town settings where he had grown up and lived as a young man, was born in Haverhill in 1807 at a site just two miles from the main gate of what was to become Winnekenni Park. With the exception of the final winters of his life, which passed in Danvers and Newburyport, Whittier spent nearly all his days in Haverhill and nearby Amesbury. Writing in *Harper's* magazine in February of 1883, George M. White commented that "It has been well said that his (Whittier's) poems might serve as a guide to Essex County." In Winnekenni Park, we find a corner of the county which reciprocates, and can still serve as a touchstone for the scenes described in the poet's country pieces.

Haverhill has changed considerably in the two centuries since Whittier grew up there in the household he described in his best work, "Snow-Bound." From minor inland seaport (Newburyport, at the mouth of the Merrimack, took over after the Revolution), it progressed to manufacturing, eventually taking its place as one of the leading shoe cities of Massachusetts. The shoe boom came to an end, though, as it did in Lynn and Brockton,

leaving a city which in 1982 received, along with nearby Lawrence, an altogether unfair designation as least favorable metropolitan area in the United States. This dubious distinction was awarded by the compilers of the *Places Rated Almanac*, who used a curiously weighted "quality of life" index to conclude that various burgs in the Sunbelt, with cockroaches who chew tobacco and third-rate symphony orchestras, somehow rate higher than a pair of quietly aging Merrimack Valley industrial towns a half-hour's drive from the BSO.

The *Places Rated Almanac* authors probably overlooked Winnekenni Park. Winnekenni (the name comes from the local Algonquin dialect, "very beautiful") is a hilly, city-owned retreat of more than 200 acres, centered upon Kenoza Lake, within a couple of miles of downtown Haverhill. It is the only park in these parts with its own castle.

AUTOMOBILE: From Boston, take Interstate Route 93 to Route 495 North. Stay on 495 until the exit for Route 110 West. Follow the signs for Haverhill. The park entrance is on Route 110 just over a mile from the exit on the left. Enter at a stone gate and park in the lot near the tennis courts.

Kenoza Lake was originally called the "Great Pond," a designation for middle-sized bodies of water apparently so popular among the early colonists that if new names had not evolved, the Commonwealth of Massachusetts would by now have had to assign numbers to all of its Great Ponds. It figures in the early history of the Haverhill area as an Indian camping ground; they especially favored the north shore, where a good many artifacts and even a skeleton, were found when the Dudley Porter Road was constructed in the early 1900s. When the town of Haverhill was besieged by the French and their Indian allies in 1708, the raiding parties came by canoe across Kenoza Lake and smaller Lake Pentucket. In more peaceful times, the lake was better known as a fishing ground for the salmon that made their way there via the tributaries of the Merrimack.

Winnekenni Park

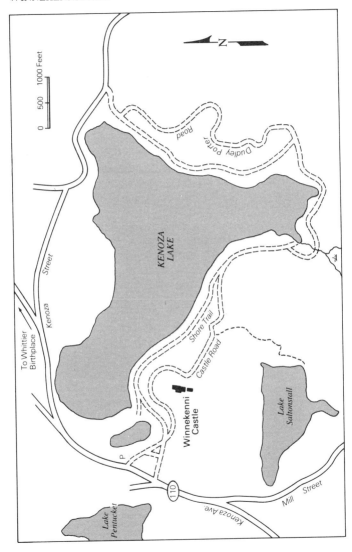

Kenoza Lake figures as a popular local recreation spot in records dating as far back as 1807. In that year, a group of Haverhill citizens bought a parcel of land on the northeastern shores of the lake (in those days still called "Great Pond") to use as a place for picnics, fishing, and boat launching. This early venture in cooperative park ownership was followed, in 1858, by an even more ambitious enterprise. This was the establishment of the Kenoza Lake Club, under whose auspices land was purchased, trees planted, and a stone lakeside clubhouse built. The 1859 dedication of the club's facilities was also the occasion for the lake's formal rechristening. None other than John Greenleaf Whittier had been asked to come up with a new name, and it was he who chose "Kenoza," an Indian word meaning "Lake of the Pickerel."

The dedication ceremony was the sort of cheery, innocent, and lofty-principled affair that our cynical age would find it hard to take with a straight face. The president of the club escorted a woman associate to a platform from which she tossed flowers into the "fair lake, whose crystal waters sparkle in the sunbeam, and whose wavelets gently kiss our feet," after which he poured a glass of wine into the lake and made its designation as Kenoza official. Next came a reading of Whittier's poem "Kenoza," composed for the occasion. It began

> As Adam did in Paradise,
>   Today the primal right we claim;
> Fair mirror of the woods and skies,
>   We give to thee a name
>
> Lake of the Pickerel! Let no more
>   The echoes answer back "Great Pond,"
> But sweet Kenoza, from thy shore
>   And watching hill beyond.

People took these things seriously in those days.

The Lake Club survived until 1890, when the Haverhill

WINNEKENNI PARK

Water Board took claim to its property as it did to the entire shoreline of Kenoza Lake during the following decade. The lake has been part of Haverhill's water supply system since 1871. Fishing and swimming are prohibited. Along the northern shore of the lake, to your left as you enter the parking lot, you will notice the system's pumping station.

The history of Winnekenni as a public park dates back to 1896, when the Haverhill Water Board turned ownership of the lake shore over to the park commission. The park could have gotten started twenty-one years earlier, had the city accepted Dr. James R. Nichols's offer of thirty acres of the property adjacent to his "castle" (of which more later) for use as a public recreation area. Officials may have been put off by a proposed covenant against picnics (was litter that big a problem before everything came in paper wrappers?) but more likely balked at his requirement that $4,000 be spent over the first year for upkeep and maintenance, and $1,000 a year thereafter.

THE WALK: There is a map of the Winnekenni hiking and ski trails posted at the parking lot on Kenoza Avenue (Route 110) where you entered the park. The main path is the Shore Trail — Dudley Porter Road, which leads around Kenoza Lake (total distance about 3 miles). Near the beginning of the Shore Trail is Castle Road, which branches off to the right and climbs uphill to the Winnekenni Castle (total distance to the castle less than ¼ mile), then continues to meet Shore Trail at the beginning of Dudley Porter Road on the lake shore. If you stay on Castle Road beyond the castle, watch for a narrower trail that veers off to the right towards Lake Saltonstall, where there is a public recreation area (swimming beach for Haverhill residents only).

The castle at Winnekenni was built in 1873–1875 by Dr. James R. Nichols, a local physician who never practiced medicine but instead spent his life researching and marketing medicines and perfecting inventions as diverse as furnaces, lamps, and soda fountains. He also founded and edited the *Journal of Chemistry*, served as a railroad president, and experimented extensively with chemical fertilizers. He lived for ninety years.

The focus of Dr. Nichols's fertilizer experiments was a farm, which he named "Winnekenni," on the western shore of Kenoza Lake. He had bought the property in 1863, and ten years later he started building what would be his summer home there. As an inspiration for his design, he chose a modern reproduction "castle" he had seen on an 1872 visit to Bath, England.

Castles, of course, are built of stone, but it was not merely a desire to ape medieval building techniques that was responsible for Dr. Nichols's interest in this material. He was an ardent campaigner for the use of stone for building, reasoning that the limitless supply of glacially deposited boulders in New England fields should be used for more than the ubiquitous stone walls that formerly divided farmers' fields and still crisscross the renascent woodlands of the region. If he had had his way, the wooden gambrel and saltbox farmsteads that characterize our landscape would have been replaced with houses made of stone.

Dr. Nichols's own stone creation, eighty-six by thirty-six feet long and four feet thick at the base, used 35,000 cubic feet of locally hewn boulders. The interior, rich in walnut, butternut, and maple, is lost to us now because fire gutted the structure in 1967.

Winnekenni Castle was the summer residence of Dr. Nichols and his family for ten years. In 1885, he sold the house and surrounding grounds to William Webb, whose wife Annie sold it to the city of Haverhill in 1895 for $28,000. During the next twenty-five years, the Haverhill park superintendent lived in a now-demolished wooden wing of the building, but the castle itself continued to deteriorate despite sporadic work on its roofs, woodwork, and mortar. The 1967 fire, set by vandals, merely finished the work that time had begun.

Conscious that Winnekenni Castle would have either to be restored or demolished and aware that the region needed an arts center, a group of Haverhill citizens formed the Winnekenni

Winnekenni Park

Foundation in 1967. Its goal has been to refurbish completely the building's interior, a sizeable task still under way as of this writing, and to make the castle and its grounds the location for cultural events and educational programs in the arts and sciences. The organization welcomes members and contributions: Winnekenni Foundation, Haverhill, MA 01830.

A visit to Winnekenni Park can be combined easily with a stopover at the birthplace of John Greenleaf Whittier. This is a sturdy, classic New England farmhouse, built in 1688 and hardly the worse for not having been built of stone as Dr. Nichols would have suggested. This is the home Whittier described in "Snow-Bound," and in it you can see the great brick hearth where the family gathered in life as in the poem, and the poet's desk as well as other original furnishings. To reach Whittier's birthplace, head back towards Interstate 495 on Route 110 but continue past the interstate entrance. Whittier Road loops and connects with 110 at both ends; the eastern end is 2.2 miles from Winnekenni parking lot. Turn left here. The Whittier House is the first building on your left. It's open Tuesday through Saturday from 10 to 5, Sundays from 1 to 5.

If Whittier and his haunts have caught your imagination, drive east into Amesbury where you can visit his home for fifty-six years at 86 Friend Street. This house is even more extensively furnished with Whittier's possessions. It is open Tuesday through Saturday, May 1 to October 31, from noon to 5. The rest of the year the house is open by appointment.

15

MIDDLETON WOODLOTS

Walking and ski touring — the Prichard and Captain Bill woodlots, components of Essex County Greenbelt's system of preserved open spaces, offer access to Boxford State Forest from the south. A developing network of trails leads through one-time farmland now grown over with mixed hardwood and coniferous forest.

WE HAVE HAD 350 years now to tame and manicure Essex County, and we have done a pretty thorough job of it. But anyone who spends much time wandering around between the Mystic and the Merrimack must invariably remark on how much open space remains in this part of Massachusetts, all of it within an hour of downtown Boston.

Many sections along the coast, of course, were for a long time too marshy to build on, and by the time construction technology had evolved so had our environmental consciousness, giving rise to coastal zone protection apparatus and wetlands preservation laws such as the Hatch Act. Other parts of Essex County have long benefited from the liberal application of private funds, which have proven to be a marvelous fertilizer for scenery — witness the legacy of Thomas Proctor, which comes down to us as the Ipswich River Wildlife Sanctuary described in Chapter 1. Finally, there are the concerted efforts of citizens who set about to acquire land to be held in public or semipublic trust. That describes the work of an organization called Essex County Greenbelt, which can count among its accomplishments the preservation of a sizeable and scenic parcel of contiguous acreage in the heart of the county's forested uplands.

During the late 1950s, the completion of Route 128 was making possible the rapid subdivision and development of the farmland and second-growth woods that girdled Boston. One developer had big plans for the drumlin known as Bald Hill, in Boxford, including building a mile-long access road through an adjacent wildlife sanctuary. A citizens' committee organized to save Bald Hill managed to get a court injunction against the road, but the fate of Bald Hill itself remained uncertain as long as it was in private hands.

The solution proposed by the committee and submitted to the state legislature was a bold one: if the committee could acquire, through purchase or gift, an area equivalent and adjacent to the 240-acre parcel which included Bald Hill, then the state would buy the hill and the entire area would be preserved as a single unit. The deal was approved and the committee, now newly organized (1961) as the Essex County Greenbelt Association, started making the necessary acquisitions. It achieved its goal and the state followed through by exercising eminent domain on the Bald Hill property — the first such use of this prerogative by the Massachusetts Department of Natural Resources for the purpose of setting aside conservation land. The new state holdings became the nucleus of Boxford State Forest. Thus, the public acquisition of this important natural resource and the founding of a local organization to advance private conservation landholding can be traced to a single preservation campaign.

Greenbelt now owns over 2,400 acres in separate parcels throughout Essex County. Appropriately, one of the organization's larger holdings borders Boxford State Forest. This is the tract made up of the Prichard and Captain Bill Woodlots in the town of Middleton — the "Middleton Woodlots," as they are collectively called. Together they comprise 135 acres of mixed upland forest — all second growth, meadows reverting to scrub, and even a white cedar bog and sections of red maple swamp.

AUTOMOBILE: From Boston, take Route 1 north to Interstate 95; stay on 95 until you see the exit for Route 62. Head

Middleton Woodlots

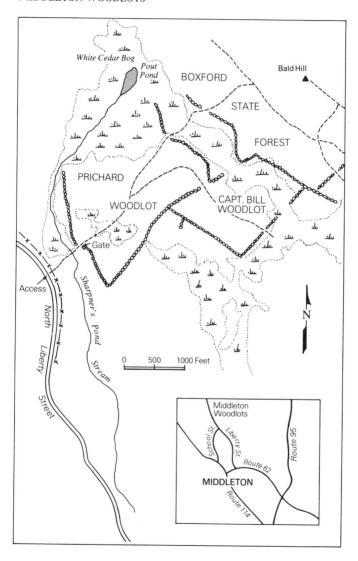

west on 62, towards Middleton. After you pass the sign that indicates that you have crossed from Danvers into Middleton, watch for Liberty Street on your right — it's the second right after you cross the Ipswich River. Follow Liberty Street past the intersection with School Street and across Boston Brook. Six tenths of a mile past Boston Brook (Liberty Street is now a gravel road), the shoulder widens sufficiently so that you can park at the entrance to a meadow on the right. Park here, but walk another hundred feet or so up the road before turning to enter the Middleton Woodlots at the beginning of an unused dirt road, also on the right, that has been blocked off with several strands of barbed wire. You should have little difficulty in getting over or under the wire.

Essex County Greenbelt acquired the Captain Bill Woodlot in 1974, and the Prichard in 1980. The Prichard lot, which is the first you will reach (see walk directions below), is a one hundred-acre tract donated by Charles Prichard, whose father bought the land, then all pasture, from Wendell Foster around 1900. These "woodlots" could not have been worthy of the name back then, since most of the area had been cleared for farming since the eighteenth century. In the 1790s, though, the remaining forests in this part of Essex County were attracting the attention of industrialists as well as of farmers seeking to expand pasturage and crop land. Daniel Porter and other Salem-based tanners bought acreage in this vicinity because of its stands of oak and hemlock, both of which yield the tannin used in treating hides. This intensive cutting of these species so long ago still accounts for their relative scarcity in some sections of the Middleton Woodlots.

The Captain Bill Woodlot came by its name for somewhat more colorful reasons — at least if the story is to be believed. Captain Bill was just that — a sea captain — who used to see Bald Hill as he sailed into Salem Harbor (remember, back when most of New England was cleared for farming you could pick out prominent natural features at a much greater distance). He decided that one day he would retire to the hill, and he did. Once

Middleton Woodlots

he got settled in he started raising carrot seeds, of all things, as a cash crop.

THE WALK: The Liberty Street access point recommended above is not actually on Greenbelt property, although entry here is permissible. The Middleton Woodlot holdings begin just beyond the cut-over land which you cross after leaving Liberty Street, where there is a wooden gate and a Greenbelt sign. If Sharpner's Pond Stream, which you will cross between the wire fence and wooden gate, is flowing at all, it can be forded. Continue past the wooden gate (not locked — just lift and replace the bar) into the Prichard Woodlot.

As you walk through the Prichard Woodlot along this main access path, you will likely notice that the pines on your left show more vigorous growth than those on your right, which are liberally interspersed with white oak, red oak, black oak, and hickory. This is because the area on the left was clearcut years ago, and the growth which succeeded is almost exclusively white pine. For a four-year period beginning in 1979, gypsy moths hit these woodlots hard — but the new pine growth to the left of the road was not affected as critically as the pines on the right, which grow amidst the white oaks that the moths prefer. Part of Greenbelt's plan for the Captain Bill Woodlot, which begins several hundred yards to the east (right), is to thin the existing stands so that more white pines will take hold. They will provide better winter cover for deer. The thinning also helps assure a source of income for Greenbelt; money from timber sales has already paid for the road improvements necessary for fire control. A pine monoculture, of course, is not the object, nor will Greenbelt make any sizeable clear-cuts. Those responsible for management also try to leave at least five dead trees per acre, for the sake of species — woodpeckers are the most visible example — dependent on them.

If you remain on the main entrance trail, you will reach

MORE COUNTRY WALKS

Boxford State Forest, recognizable by the looming outline of Bald Hill straight ahead. Or, you can take either of two right-hand turnoffs: both lead into the Captain Bill Woodlot and loop back to the main trail along the southern periphery of the state forest. The white cedar bog lies off to the left of the main trail, a little over a half-mile in from Liberty Street. Be careful if you visit the bog; like all true bogs, it consists of a mass of dense organic material floating on water, and it is possible to break through.

A note on trail markings: as of this writing, there are blazes of different colors — generally orange, yellow, and blue — dating from different attempts at imposing order on the trail system. Greenbelt is working on a streamlined marking scheme in which blue will indicate routes leading away from the Liberty Street access point, and yellow will show that you are on your way back. If you bring a compass, remember that heading in a general southwesterly direction will bring you to Liberty Street. A USGS topographical map (South Groveland, Georgetown, and Reading quadrangle) is also useful.

The Middleton Woodlots are a fine place to enjoy spring ferns and wildflowers — early in the season, hepatica (liverwort) and columbine are among the species in bloom. Birders are particularly attracted to the area during spring and fall migrations, and to observe raptors such as the red-shouldered hawk and barred owl, diurnal-nocturnal counterparts who sometimes make their nests in the same tree. (Greenbelt is always interested in reports of plants and animals seen in the Middleton Woodlots or at other properties; these sightings help provide the necessary documentation for species inventories.)

In addition to the inventories, Greenbelt prepares management plans for each of its holdings. Day-to-day supervision is the charge of regional monitors; there is one in each municipality in which Greenbelt has property. The monitors, in turn, assign informal oversight tasks to local volunteers, so that the

MIDDLETON WOODLOTS

appearance of management from afar is avoided. Use regulations predicated upon traditional patterns also help assure good community relations: if a Greenbelt property has been hunted historically, as have the Middleton Woodlots, hunting may continue. Except for temporary closings of some areas relative to nesting seasons and other management considerations, hikers and cross-country skiers are always welcome. The only strict, universal prohibition is against motorized vehicles.

For more information on the Middleton Woodlots or other Greenbelt properties, or about joining the organization, write Essex County Greenbelt, 82 Eastern Avenue, Essex, MA 01929.

16

IPSWICH TO NEWBURYPORT: THE B&M EASTERN DIVISION

Walking or ski touring — follow the tracks for 11 miles from one old North Shore town to another, along the way enjoying seldom-seen perspectives of Essex woods and marshes and making some observations about the construction and maintenance of this now nearly abandoned rail route. If you wish, spend the night in a Newburyport inn and return the following day.

IN THE 1640s, an Indian or an English colonist could follow a path from the village of Agawam, later Ipswich, to the tiny Parker River settlement of Newbury and scarcely encounter another living soul, let alone even the simplest of conveyances, throughout the whole of his ten-mile journey. Today, that path has been worn smooth, widened, and asphalted, and is known as Route 1A. But it is still possible to walk through the woods and vast salt marshes that separate these ancient Essex towns, along a route less frequented even than the path traveled by the early settlers. The secret of recapturing this seventeenth-century pedestrian solitude is to take a page from the nineteenth and follow the all-but-abandoned tracks of the Boston and Maine Railroad's Eastern Division.

This is the longest of the walks in this book and for anyone keen on the pleasure of not simply taking a country ramble but actually getting from one place to another, it is easily the most rewarding. There are public transportation connections at both

ends, good food and accommodations in Newburyport, and the
simplest of directions: a continuous trail blazed by two
ribbons of steel.

*PUBLIC TRANSPORTATION: Take a Boston and Maine/
MBTA train from Boston's North Station to Ipswich. The trip
takes about an hour. Before leaving, call Greyhound to
verify schedules for your return by bus from Newburyport,
unless you plan to go back the way you came.*

*AUTOMOBILE: Not really recommended, but if you wish to
drive you can leave your car in the station lot in downtown
Ipswich and simply retrace your route along the tracks, or
you can use two cars and spot one in Newburyport. To get to
Ipswich, take Route 1 north from Boston. Turn right at the
second traffic light after the Topsfield Fairgrounds onto
Ipswich Road. Follow Ipswich Road for 6 miles. When you
reach downtown Ipswich, turn left onto Washington Street.
The train station is one block away at the intersection of
Washington and Hammett Streets.*

The right-of-way between Ipswich and Newburyport originally belonged to the Eastern Railroad, an enterprise so conservative that as late as 1871 it still did not use the telegraph. On August 26th of that year, the absence of telegraphic orders on the Eastern caused the great Revere Disaster, in which one passenger train rear-ended another and twenty-nine people were killed. The accident helped bring about a clamor for much-needed railroad safety reforms, but it also spelled the beginning of the end for the Eastern: the road's fortunes declined over the next decade, and in 1884 it was swallowed by the up-and-coming Boston and Maine. The coastal route north of Boston became the B&M's Eastern Division. It extended beyond Ipswich and Newburyport to Portsmouth, New Hampshire, and Kittery, Maine, before forking at Conway Junction, Maine, into routes leading to Portland and the White Mountains.

Ipswich to Newburyport

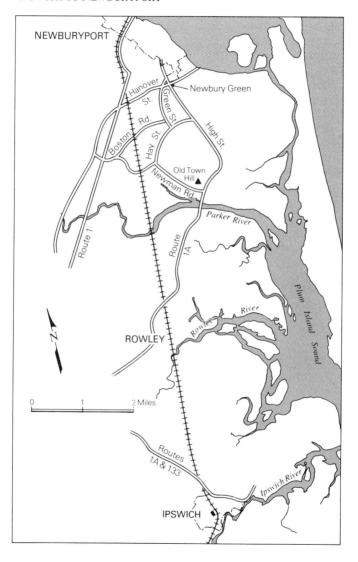

The B&M, which operates the Massachusetts Bay Transportation Authority's commuter rail routes on the North Shore, stopped running passenger trains between Ipswich and Newburyport in the mid-1970s. Although there is some support for restoring service north of Ipswich (it would take some track work, as you will see), the road is now used only for an occasional freight — once a week, perhaps, or even less. But, when walking along any rail route, no matter how infrequent the service, you should stay alert for train sounds. The major portion of this route, however, is paralleled by a gravel path wide enough for a vehicle, so there is no need to walk directly on the tracks except at the Parker River crossing (see below).

THE WALK: Get off the train at Ipswich and simply follow the tracks out of town, heading north the way the train would if this were not the end of the line. If you are parking in the station lot, north is to your right.

For the first mile or so out of Ipswich, the views are mostly of the backs of houses and an occasional small factory or auto graveyard. Don't worry; it gets a lot better. While you are waiting for more pleasant vistas to open up, you can learn a bit about railroad construction by "reading" the rails and ties alongside the path. The name of the manufacturer of the rail, the date it was made, and its weight per yard are stamped into the steel, at intervals of several feet. The Eastern Division of the B&M is a real hodgepodge: at different places along the track you'll see *85-AS BS* Co. *Lackawanna OH IV 1925 85-ASCE*, indicating, in part, that Bethlehem Steel made the rail in 1925, and that it was certified at 85 lbs. per yard by the American Society of Civil Engineers; or *Krupp O.H.V. 1926 ASCE 85 Germany*, meaning that the B&M was taking advantage of the low value of the Weimar mark and, inadvertently, keeping the steel barons of the Ruhr in practice for bigger things. See if you can also locate the rail made in Buffalo in 1905 — it's about four miles out of Ipswich.

Ipswich to Newburyport

There is also a way to tell the age of the wooden ties, if you can find any that still have the little metal buttons stamped into their surfaces. These are about ⅜ inch across and bear two digits — the year the tie was laid. There are some ties along this route marked *49* and some whose markers read *41*; this should tell you a little about why they're in such decrepit shape. Actually, the real wonder is that so many are still sound. Creosoting and good drainage help.

The disparity between rail and tie ages indicates that ties were replaced beneath existing rail. Nowadays, this job is done by integrated machines that lift rails and spikes, saw through and discard rotted ties, slip new ties into place, and even clean and tamp the gravel ballast. When these ties were laid, the work was done by crews of men who yanked spikes with long crowbars, loosened the ballast and subsoil with shovels, and lifted lengths of rail with powerful, manually operated jacks. Then the old ties would be removed with a tool resembling giant ice tongs, and the new ones slid in and tamped firmly into place. Once the tie plates were positioned, one worker would warn the others to stand back while he tripped the jack and let the rail slam down. Then came the hard part: driving the spikes home with heavy, narrow-headed spike hammers. The trick was to hit the spike heads cleanly and avoid striking the rail, a mistake which would cause the fillings in your teeth to rattle.

About two miles out of Ipswich, the salt marshes begin to grow more expansive, especially off to the right. They are occasionally interrupted by stands of hardwoods; the gently curving outline of the crowns of such a stand often betray the presence of a glacial drumlin beneath. The thickets along the borders of woods and marsh are frequently cruised by raptors looking for prey, and at some point along this route you will probably be able to follow the circling flight of a red-shouldered or rough-legged hawk.

At about 2½ miles out, an occasional heather bush growing between the tracks indicates that the infrequent freights pass by just enough to keep the shrubs clipped back squarely from the inside of the rail but not quite enough to keep the middle entirely clear. Also in this area, where the tracks cross narrow streams on a pair of wooden bridges with Rockport granite foundations, a steady, ubiquitous trickling will remind you that the ocean is not far away — these rivulets respond to the tides, and the sound you hear is that of the circulatory system of a living salt marsh.

Just over 3½ miles from Ipswich, you will cross the Rowley River. Remember that this is a railroad bridge, and that you have to step on the cross planks, which are actually just extended ties (there isn't enough room between them for a person to fall through, but you could twist an ankle if you step carelessly.) Here is where the grand sweep of the Rowley marshes really opens up to your right. You are looking eastward to the southern reaches of Plum Island, across land once valued for its crop of salt hay. The nineteenth-century luminist artist Fitz Hugh Lane knew these marshes well, and painted them much as they still appear.

Markedly different terrain comes into view about 4½ miles out of Ipswich. Here you can see where the railroad builders had to blast through exposed ledge, especially in the area where Route 1A crosses the tracks on a circa-1930s concrete bridge.

About five miles from Ipswich, signs indicate that the marshes and wooded hillocks to the west (left) are part of a designated wildlife management area, in which hunting, fishing, and trapping are permitted. In the fall you may well encounter hunters along the track either on foot or in vehicles, and wearing bright colors is advisable. This stretch, however, does not appear to be hunted heavily.

You are now past the halfway point. Having come about 6 miles from Ipswich, you can look ahead to the Newburyport water tower, slightly off to the right. After another half mile the tracks reach the Parker River; the first English settlers of Newbury arrived at its mouth in 1635. *Be careful* when you cross the Parker River bridge. The ties beneath the rails are soundest, so this is where you should walk.

As you emerge again into open marshland, just after passing

IPSWICH TO NEWBURYPORT

beneath an old iron trestle some 7 miles out of Ipswich, look off to the right. The high point of land is Old Town Hill, Newbury, described in Chapter 12 of this book. Several hundred yards to your left, the traffic along Route 1, the old Newburyport Turnpike, will be barely visible. This final stretch of marshland, hemmed in by gentle hills and within sight of the church spires of Newbury and Newburyport, is perhaps the loveliest along the Eastern Division route. The colors are at their best in late spring and early to mid-autumn, when the always-subtle palette of the marsh contrasts with the brighter tones of the quickening or dying foliage along its periphery. It is a place at once of the coast and of the inland countryside, and one which — this rusted railroad aside — has hardly changed since Europeans first set eyes on it three and a half centuries ago.

The first road you reach after passing Old Town Hill will be Hay Street, Newbury; after another half mile, you'll come to Boston Road, so named because in colonial times it was part of the main route between Newburyport and Boston. If you turn right here, you can follow Boston Road to Green Street, and then turn left for the two-mile walk past Newbury Green into Newburyport. If you choose this route, keep an eye out for the eighteenth-century stone marker that tells the distance to Boston, identified simply as "B." It will be on your right alongside a field just before you get to the Green, roughly opposite the Colonial Pharmacy.

If you prefer to follow the tracks a little longer, continue to Hanover Street (the next grade crossing) and turn right. Walk along Hanover Street to Green Street at Newbury Green, then turn left to follow High Street into Newburyport. As you walk along High Street, you'll pass the First Parish Church of Newbury, descended from the church of the earliest settlers; the church's ancient burial ground; a produce stand belonging to the three-hundred-year-old Arrowhead Farm; the circa-1653 Coffin House; and the Cushing House, the museum of the Historical Society of Old Newbury. Turn right at State Street to reach the main business district.

Ipswich to Newburyport

Just as in colonial times, you have walked a considerable distance from one town to another. And, as in those days, your first thoughts are likely to be of food and lodging. Newburyport offers more possibilities than most cities of its size. Two good restaurants at the pricier end of the scale are *Scandia* and *Ten Center Street*; neither requires a tie. The *Grog* and *Arriba* restaurants, both under the same roof on Middle Street, offer pub-style and Mexican dining respectively, at modest prices. For a good night's sleep, try either the Garrison Inn (expensive) or the Morrill Place, a charming inn in a big Federalist house on High Street. Breakfast is served, the rooms are furnished with antiques, and the prices are moderate. All of these establishments except the last are right downtown, and the Morrill Place is about eight blocks past State Street at the corner of High and Johnson.

Unless you have a car in Newburyport or are walking back to Ipswich, the best way back to Boston is by Greyhound bus. Buses depart several times each day from a station near the Port Plaza shopping mall on Storey Avenue, about 2½ miles west of downtown. Don't forget to call Greyhound for schedules when you plan your trip.

17

WHITNEY AND THAYER WOODS

Walking and ski touring — a circuit of approximately 2½ miles, one of many that are possible within this Trustees of Reservations preserve of nearly eight hundred acres in Cohasset and Hingham. The woods cover a rocky, gently ascending terrain once farmed by South Shore yeomen and since reverted to forest.

WHEN CAPTAIN JOHN SMITH sailed into Cohasset Harbor in 1614, one of the first local features he might have noticed was Turkey Hill, a 187-foot drumlin standing just inland, brooding over the forested, as yet unpenetrated Massachusetts coast.

Today, you can climb Turkey Hill and look the other way, out over the harbor Smith was allegedly the first European to see, around which has since grown up one of the prettiest New England coastal towns. The hill is the highest point in a 799-acre forest tract called the Whitney and Thayer Woods, owned and managed by the Trustees of Public Reservations.

These woods, of course, are not the ones John Smith peered into from the deck of his ship. By 1633, Englishmen had settled and begun farming in Hingham; fourteen years later, they were beginning to spread south into Cohasset. In those early days, Cohasset — still part of the town of Hingham — was used mainly as a source of wood and salt hay. With the first apportioning of farmland, or "division," clearing the forest became more extensive and systematic.

Cohasset's second division was undertaken in 1670 and 1671 under the direction of Joshua Fisher, a surveyor from Dedham.

MORE COUNTRY WALKS

This division involved the land that we now call the Whitney and Thayer Woods. Fisher believed that everyone being assigned land should have a share of each type of the local terrain, with the size of the apportioned lots to vary with the status of the townsman as defined by his existing holdings. The smallest of the lots carved out in the Whitney and Thayer Woods area were one rod, or a little over sixteen feet, in width, with lengths that ran much farther. This does not make a very practical farm. The local yeomen got down to swapping, and managed to arrive at a patchwork of fields and pasture that looked more like a checkerboard than a pin-striped suit. The neat, parallel stone walls that you see there today are the remains of their property boundaries. Originally the walls were closer to chest-high, since this land was mostly sheep pastures and sheep are more acrobatic than cows. These stone fences are lower now, but in their squat permanence they may well convince you that when the sun goes out, the last things standing will be one Great Wall on one side of the earth and ten thousand little ones on the other.

As recently as the 1870s, Cohasset people could look from one side of these "woods" clear across to the other, with hardly a tree to block their view. Around then, though, farms began to be abandoned, and the fallow land quickly reverted to birch and white pine. The area was already forest in 1933, when 640 acres of former Whitney family property was donated by the Whitney Woods Association to the Trustees of Reservations (the "Thayer" in the reservation's name is due to the 1943 donation by Mrs. Ezra Thayer of 28 acres in Hingham, making this a two-town property). Other purchases and donations have brought the Trustees' holdings to their present size. The reservation also includes the Bancroft Bird Sanctuary, a 25-acre tract on the other side of Route 3A near its intersection with King Street. The Whitney and Thayer Woods are actually part of a much larger open area, as the reservation borders the 2,700-acre Wompatuck State Park, with its forests, campgrounds, and self-guided nature trails. (Call 749-7160 for Wompatuck information.)

WHITNEY AND THAYER WOODS

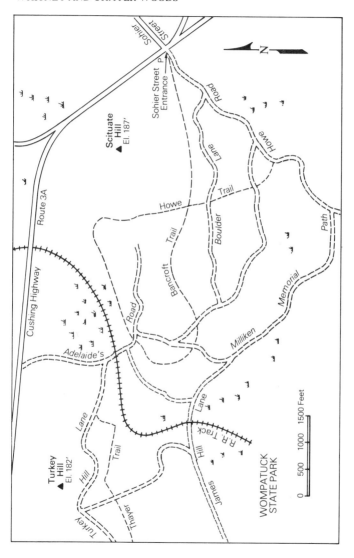

Those original succeeding stands of white pine and birch have since been joined by red maple, ash, oak, and hemlock. At the foot of Turkey Hill, near the old railroad tracks, there is also a stand of holly trees that is the largest in North America.

AUTOMOBILE: From Boston, take the Southeast Expressway to the turnoff for Route 3A. Follow 3A south through Weymouth and Hingham into Cohasset. At the intersection of 3A and Sohier Street, look for the Trustees of Public Reservations sign and the entrance to the Whitney and Thayer Woods on your right. Parking is available just inside the entrance.

THE WALK: Howe's Road heads directly into the woods from the main entrance at Sohier Street and Route 3A. Virtually all of the reservation's trails branch to the right off this dirt road; few, however, are well marked as of this writing. Use the map in this book or obtain one from the Trustees of Reservations, 224 Adams Street, Milton, MA 02186. For an interesting circuit of under two miles, take Howe's Road ⅓ mile to Boulder Lane and turn right. Follow Boulder Lane past Bigelow Boulder, a 200-ton granite erratic. Continue on Boulder Lane to the Howe Trail, about ¼ mile past the boulder, and turn left. The Howe Trail, named for Cohasset physician Oliver Howe, an AMC member dedicated to Whitney Woods Trail upkeep, brings you back to Howe's Road in the vicinity (to the right on Howe's Road) of the large "Rooster Rock" formation, where several small rocks hold up an enormous boulder, and Ode's Den, named for Theodore Pritchard, an old man who in the 1820s quarreled with his family, left home, and came here to live beneath a rock ledge. He eventually froze to death. Return to the main entrance by turning left from the Howe Trail onto Howe's Road.

If you turn right at the intersection of Boulder Lane and the Howe Trail, you can follow the latter to the Mystery Millstone on the edge of the reservation near the foot of Scituate

WHITNEY AND THAYER WOODS

Hill, just before the trail veers to the left. The millstone was probably being cut here many years ago for use at another site, when its maker realized it was flawed with a major crack and abandoned it. Stonecutting, by the way, was once a prominent local industry. There was even a pink granite quarry in the Woods that served Louis Comfort Tiffany's firm as a source of lamp bases and other ornamental objects.

If you continue on Howe's Trail past the millstone, you will reach Adelaide's Road just short of a little-used railroad track. Turn right on Adelaide's Road, cross the track, and bear left at the fork to reach Turkey Hill, from the top of which you can enjoy the view of Cohasset harbor. Return the way you came, or via any of the other roads and trails indicated on the map. If you become disoriented, listen for the sounds of traffic on Route 3A. The main entrance to the Woods will be to your right if you reach this highway.

One of the more pleasant trails through Whitney and Thayer Woods is the Milliken Memorial Path, which branches off to the right of Howe's Road near the boundary of Wompatuck State Park, just over a mile from the Woods entrance. Some sixty years ago, this was one of the favorite carriage roads of a Mrs. Milliken, and upon her death her husband donated money for landscaping and ornamental plantings along its route. The landscape architect hired for the job was Harlan Kelsey, who had recently worked on the Blue Ridge Parkway in Virginia and North Carolina. Still influenced by his southern commission, Kelsey graced the Milliken Path with azalea, rhododendron, and Carolinian hemlock, much of which survives and may still be enjoyed in season.

Whitney and Thayer Woods, Cohasset, Massachusetts is open from sunrise to sunset throughout the year. Contact the Trustees of Reservations (address above) for further information.

18

DOGTOWN

Walking and ski touring — follow prerevolutionary pathways for 4 miles through a strange and desolate section of Gloucester and Rockport and past the ancient cellar holes that are the lone reminders of a vanished settlement.

FINISHED WITH ITS broad northward arc through the future, America's Technology Highway — Route 128 — fizzles out within a stone's throw of the seventeenth century, near a place where Lear's mad scene could be played without investing a penny in sets. Dogtown is part moorland, part melancholy forest; it is a corner of Cape Ann (its center, actually) where no one has lived for over a century and a half, and where the boulders speak in aphorisms.

Dogtown is shared by Gloucester and Rockport, and it comprises roughly five square miles of uninhabited territory: wooded upland, broken plateau, freshwater marsh. But Dogtown was not always forsaken by Cape Ann's human population. For over a century, the paths you will walk here were roads, and the bramble-filled cellar holes you may come across were the foundations of houses. Dogtown is one of those places that became settled and then unsettled. It is a ghost town.

In several chapters in this book, you will find references to "divisions" of land made during the early colonial period. These divisions were part of the sequence of land distribution that came about as the population grew. In the first division — often early in the seventeenth century in this part of New England — land near the town center was apportioned, with

outlying acreage held in reserve until later generations required
it for tilling and pasturage. These consequent divisions of what
was, for the time being, an "endless" supply of land no doubt
enabled primogeniture and the universal pursuit of agriculture to
coexist. When the land ran out, of course, younger heirs headed
west or turned to trade.

The late Charles Mann, a local historian, suggested that the
part of Gloucester which we now call Dogtown came under
division in 1719. People moved there, built houses, and farmed.
But when the Revolution was over and unrestricted trade and
fishing were possible, the attraction of coastal enterprises lured
most of Dogtown's residents away from their farms. As un-
forgiving as the North Atlantic can be, it is at least as quick to
yield a living as the thin, rocky soil of Cape Ann. Who remained
in Dogtown? Their description depends on whom you read. For
the most part they were poor, unemployable by reason of age or
disposition, and often inclined to drink. (They drank hard cider
and cheap rum rather than brandy and Madeira, which made
their antics all the more worthy of censure.) A number of them
were elderly spinsters and widows, scratching along in a trickle-
down economy where not much ever trickled down. If you fit
that description in the eighteenth century, you were as likely as
not to be stuck with the name of witch — especially if your
demeanor was no sweeter than your circumstances might
warrant.

Here we have the reason behind the silly and superficial
stories that Dogtown occasionally engenders, set pieces about
dark doings and wizened crones that have little if any basis in
historical fact. The real inhabitants of Dogtown in the days of its
decline were just a bunch of poor unfortunates, the "bag ladies"
of their day, as one amateur historian has put it. (The name of
the town, by the way, appears to have come from packs of wild
dogs who descended from the pets and guardians that were
abandoned as the old recluses died, moved, or were carted off to
the poorhouse. The dogs are not there today.)

Dogtown's last citizen made that trip to the poorhouse in

Dogtown

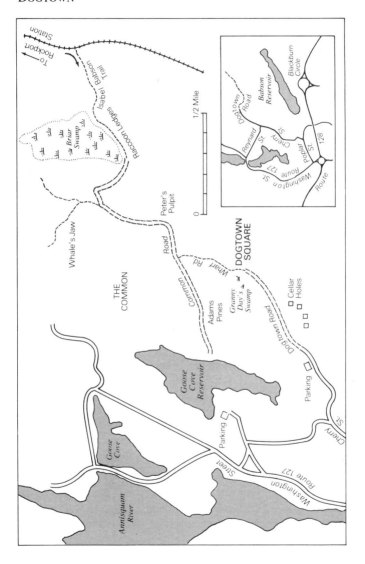

1830, and no one has lived there permanently since. The houses collapsed, burned, were dismantled for firewood or otherwise disappeared, and the place grew more and more to resemble a setting for Walpurgis Night rituals: topography, too, can mark a spot as suspect in the eyes of the virtuous.

By the early twentieth century, Dogtown had become the wild, lonely place that we know today, whose forlorn beauty was captured in the spare, realistic landscapes of Marsden Hartley, a painter who worked in the first decades of this century. It was always popular with people like Hartley who appreciated solitary rambles through woods and overgrown meadows. Another such person was Roger Babson, who perhaps more than anyone else is responsible for the preservation of Dogtown as we know it today.

Roger Babson was a descendant of one of Gloucester's oldest families. His first American forebear was Isabel Babson, a widow with a small son who turned up in the little fishing village in the middle of the seventeenth century and went to work as a midwife. She was paid by the town for some of her work, which involved rudimentary gynecology and pediatrics as well as the delivery of babies. Roger Babson, her wealthy and prominent descendant, saw to it that the maternity wing of the local hospital was named for her, as is the small library — devoted exclusively to family health care — on Main Street in Gloucester.

Roger Babson himself was a financial whiz who earned a reputation that served him all his life by successfully predicting the stock market crash of 1929. Babson College in Wellesley, Massachusetts, is named for him. Having made his name and his fortune, he could afford a few eccentricities. He wrote books on an astounding variety of subjects, including the history of Gloucester; ran as a candidate for president on the temperance ticket and wrote that party's 1940 platform; supported research into the possibility of overcoming gravity; and bought well over 1,000 acres of Dogtown, which he turned over to the city of Gloucester to use as part of its watershed (Babson Reservoir was filled in 1930). And, he sent stonecutters out to carve on the Dogtown boulders.

DOGTOWN

The Babson-sponsored Dogtown carvings fall into two categories. As a local history buff, he wanted to identify sites connected with various Dogtown events or previously existing structures, and consequently had a series of numbers carved into rocks at the relevant locations. If you are interested in matching descriptions to the numbers you may find (many are overgrown or otherwise hard to spot), inquire at the Gloucester Public Library. The other Babson carvings need no code or key, and are much easier to see. These are the pithy mottoes — often no more than one word — chiseled into the faces of many of Dogtown's more prominent boulders. A sampling:

>*Loyalty*
>*Kindness*
>*Spiritual Power*
>*Integrity*
>*Get A Job*
>*Ideas*
>*Never Try Never Win*
>*Study*
>*Help Mother*
>*If Work Stops, Values Decline.*

It's fun to wander through Dogtown, keeping track of these admonishments as you come across them. There are about twenty or twenty-one, and they give you an idea of what Easter Island would look like if it had been settled by Calvinists.

PUBLIC TRANSPORTATION: One of the points of access into Dogtown is the B&M railroad terminal in Rockport. Take a Rockport train out of Boston's North Station (don't forget to check return times and keep an eye on your watch while you're out in the woods), get off at the last stop, and walk along the tracks to the Isabel Babson Trail as described below.

AUTOMOBILE: From Boston, take Route 1 to Route 128

More Country Walks

north. Follow 128 into Gloucester, and get on Route 127 heading north towards Annisquam and Rockport. There are several places to park and begin your walk — including, of course, the train station in Rockport. The two parking areas on the northern fringes of Dogtown are off Cherry Street and Dee Avenue (the latter is near Goose Cove Reservoir); the directions here are for the Cherry Street access point. These parking areas are well out of sight of heavily traveled roads, so lock your car and don't leave anything valuable in view. Some of the local adolescents don't take Babson's carvings seriously.

Turn off Route 128 and onto Route 127 at Grant Circle. Follow 127 for 0.9 mile to Reynard Street and turn right. Turn left onto Cherry Street at the next intersection, bear right at the upcoming fork, and continue until you get to the wide place in the road beyond which driving would be problematic.

If you can arrange it, try spotting cars here and at the Rockport train station. That way you won't have to backtrack or get lost trying to work out a loop route.

THE WALK: The following describes the approximately 3½- to 4-mile (one way) route from the Rockport train station to the Cherry Street parking area. It can easily be followed in reverse. There are many other trails through Dogtown, in varying states of repair; if you are serious about exploring the area, use a topographical map and compass, or take along a copy of The Wilds of Cape Ann *(see bibliography), which contains a serviceable fold-out map of Dogtown.*

Follow the B&M tracks (keep well away from the rails!) as if you were backtracking towards Boston. Approximately half a mile from the station, just beyond a curve that puts the station out of view, the Isabel Babson Trail slabs up the bank to the right. It may be tricky to spot in the summer. At first the trail is blazed with orange and green markings; later, they are all orange. You will pass through a boulder-strewn area

NEVER TRY
NEVER WIN

called the Raccoon Ledges, and then across the top of an old stone dam, a WPA project now surrounded by dry land. After crossing the dam, bear to the right, continuing to follow the orange blazes. Look for a right turnoff, blazed with double orange dots *to reach the rock formation known as the Whale's Jaw.*

The Whale's Jaw is a huge split boulder, aptly named, standing 191 feet above sea level. It is a popular spot for picnics and, if you feel up to climbing it, a good vantage point especially when the trees are not in leaf.

Return to the Isabel Babson Trail via the short Whale's Jaw connector and turn right. This is the Common Road; it will take you uphill to another prominent boulder called Peter's Pulpit. Stay on the Common Road as it veers to the right; about 1,000 feet beyond Peter's Pulpit, Wharf Road leads off to the left. Wharf Road is blazed with orange and green dots. It was named for Abraham Wharf, who lived here until 1814 in a long-vanished house marked by boulder 24 on the left side of the path. Follow Wharf Road for its half-mile length, much of which is bordered by wetlands on either side. Mosquito repellent — lots of it — is a must here in summer.

Granny Day's Swamp, on your right as you approach "Dogtown Square" at the end of Wharf Road, surrounds tiny Boulder Pond. This is a small kettle hole, half-filled with glacial erratics, which shows some evidence of bog characteristics in its border growth of sphagnum moss. This is a quiet, almost gloomy spot, and if you are taken by the spooky side of the Dogtown mystique you might find it reminiscent of these lines from Poe's "Dream-Land":

> By the grey woods, — by the swamp
> Where the toad and the newt encamp, —
> By the dismal tarns and pools

Dogtown

> Where dwell the Ghouls, —
> By each spot the most unholy —
> In each nook most melancholy, —

Wharf Road takes you into Dogtown Square, which, like the open space around the Whale's Jaw, is somewhat of a trail interchange and popular resting spot. It was around the Square that many of Dogtown's houses once stood. Dogtown Road, which leads off at a southwesterly angle ahead and to the right of where you entered the Square, has old cellar holes along both sides, mostly on the right as you approach from this direction. All are within forty feet of the road; look for narrow, usually overgrown paths, or for Babson's numbered boulders. Most of the cellar holes are identifiable only as brush-filled depressions, and none is as large as a modern house foundation.

Follow Dogtown Road for about 0.75 mile to reach the area known as Gronblad's Pit, after an old gravel pit, where the Cherry Street parking area is located.

Most of Dogtown is owned by the city of Gloucester, either as part of the watershed or as conservation land. Although there are some private holdings along Dogtown Road, trespass should not be a problem.

BIBLIOGRAPHY

AMC Massachusetts and Rhode Island Trail Guide. Fifth Edition. Boston: Appalachian Mountain Club, 1982.

Bacon, Edwin M. *Walks and Rides in the Country About Boston*. Boston: Appalachian Mountain Club/ Houghton Mifflin, 1898.

Charters, Ann. *Kerouac: A Biography*. San Francisco: Straight Arrow Books, 1973.

Codman, John Thomas. *Brook Farm: Historic and Personal Memoirs*. Boston: Arena Publishing Company, 1894.

Federal Writers Project. *Massachusetts: A Guide to Its Places and People*. (American Guide Series) Boston: Houghton Mifflin, 1937. (Reprint edition with introduction by Jane Holtz Kay, New York: Pantheon, 1983.)

First Annual Report of the Lynn Park Commissioners. Lynn, Massachusetts, 1890.

Second Annual Report of the Lynn Park Commissioners. Lynn, Massachusetts, 1891.

Fisher, Alan. *AMC Guide to Country Walks Near Boston*. Boston: Appalachian Mountain Club, 1976.

BIBLIOGRAPHY

Freeman, Donald C. *The Story of Winnekenni, 1640-1976*. Haverhill, Massachusetts: The Board of Directors of the Winnekenni Foundation, 1976.

Freeman, Donald C., et al, eds. *Whittier and Whittierland: Portrait of a Poet and His World*. Amesbury, Massachusetts: Trustees of the John Greenleaf Whittier Homestead, 1976.

Gard, Barbara. "Belle Isle: A Salt Marsh in a City." Unpublished thesis submitted to Tufts University, May 1984.

Garland, Joseph E. *Boston's Gold Coast: The North Shore, 1890-1929*. Boston: Little, Brown and Co., 1981.

Garland, Joseph E. *Boston's North Shore*. Boston: Little, Brown and Co., 1978.

Garland, Joseph E. *The Gloucester Guide: A Retrospective Ramble*. Gloucester, Massachusetts: Gloucester 350th Anniversary Celebration, 1973.

Gifford, Barry. *Kerouac's Town*. Berkeley, California: Creative Arts Book Company, 1977.

Ingersoll, Ernest. *Down East Latch Strings; or, Seashore, Lakes and Mountains by the Boston and Maine Railroad*. Boston: Passenger Department, Boston and Maine Railroad, 1887.

Kales, Emily and David. *All About the Boston Harbor Islands*. Boston: Herman Publishing Inc., 1976.

Kerouac, Jack. *Doctor Sax*. New York: Grove Press, 1959.

Kerouac, Jack. *Visions of Gerard*. New York: McGraw-Hill, 1976.

Mellow, James R. *Nathaniel Hawthorne in His Times*. Boston: Houghton Mifflin, 1980.

Pfeiffer, Marion. *The Mills at Broadmoor, 1696-1976*. Natick, Massachusetts: Massachusetts Audubon Society/Natick Bicentennial Commission, 1976.

Pickard, Samuel T. *Whittier-Land: A Handbook of North Essex.* Cambridge: The Riverside Press, 1904 (reprinted by the Trustees of the John Greenleaf Whittier Homestead, Amesbury, Massachusetts, 1974).

Pope, Eleanor. *The Wilds of Cape Ann: A Guide to the Natural Areas of Essex, Gloucester, and Rockport, Massachusetts.* Gloucester and Rockport, Massachusetts: Resources for Cape Ann/Essex County Ecology Center, Inc., 1981.

Primack, Mark. "Charles Eliot: Genius of the Massachusetts Landscape." *Appalachia*, June 15, 1982, pp. 80-88.

Scheller, William G. "Plum Island." (Ipswich River) *Sanctuary*, Aug.-Sept., 1981, pp. 9-12.

Scheller, William G. "Pumping Dry the River." (Ipswich River) *Sanctuary*, Sept.-Oct., 1982, pp. 10-11.

Seashore, Lakes and Mountains. Boston: Passenger Department, Boston and Maine Railroad, 1886.

Snow, Edward Rowe. *The Islands of Boston Harbor, 1630-1971.* New York: Dodd, Mead, 1971.

Tree, Christina. *How New England Happened.* Boston: Little, Brown and Co., 1976.

ABOUT THE AMC

The Appalachian Mountain Club is a non-profit volunteer organization of over 30,000 members. Centered in the northeastern United States with headquarters in Boston, its membership is worldwide. The AMC was founded in 1876, making it the oldest and largest organization of its kind in America. Its existence has been committed to conserving, developing, and managing dispersed outdoor recreational opportunities for the public in the Northeast. Its efforts in the past have endowed it with a significant public trust and its volunteers and staff today maintain that tradition.

Twelve regional chapters from Maine to Pennsylvania, some sixty committees, and hundreds of volunteers supported by a dedicated professional staff join in administering the Club's wide-ranging programs. Besides volunteer organized and led expeditions, these include research, backcountry management, trail and shelter construction and maintenance, conservation, and outdoor education. The Club operates a unique system of eight alpine huts in the White Mountains, a base camp and public information center at Pinkham Notch, New Hampshire, a public service facility in the Catskill Mountains of New York, five full service camps, four self-service camps, and nine campgrounds, all open to the public. Its Boston headquarters houses not only a public information center but also the largest mountaineering library and research facility in the U. S. The Club also conducts leadership workshops, mountain search and rescue, and a youth opportunity program for disadvantaged urban young people. The AMC publishes guidebooks, maps, and America's oldest mountaineering journal, *Appalachia*.

We invite you to join and share in the benefits of membership. Membership brings a subscription to the monthly bulletin *Appalachia*; discounts on publications and at the huts and camps managed by the Club; notices of trips and programs; and, association with chapters and their meetings and activities. Most important, membership offers the opportunity to support and share in the major public service efforts of the Club.

Membership is open to the general public upon completion of an application form and payment of an initiation fee and annual dues. Information on membership as well as the names and addresses of the secretaries of local chapters may be obtained by writing to: The Appalachian Mountain Club, 5 Joy Street, Boston, Massachusetts 02108, or calling during business hours 617-523-0636.

AMC Country Walks books . . . for busy city dwellers who want country outings without spending half the day getting there and coming back.

* *20 walks in and near the city, each with directions, maps and photos*
* *natural and social history, local legends and anecdotes*
* *handy, pocket size*

Country Walks Near Boston, Alan Fisher
$6.95 pb * 180 pages * 0-910146-07-1

Country Walks Near New York, William G. Scheller
$6.95 pb * 200 pages * 0-910146-29-2

Country Walks Near Baltimore, Alan Fisher
$7.95 pb * 214 pages * 0-910146-36-5

Country Walks Near Montreal, William G. Scheller
$7.95 pb * 152 pages * 0-910146-40-3 English ed. *
0-910146-46-2 French ed.

Country Walks Near Philadelphia, Alan Fisher
$7.95 pb * 180 pages * 0-910146-42-X

Country Walks in Connecticut, Susan D. Cooley
$6.95 pb * 218 pages * 0-910146-41-1

Country Walks Near Washington, Alan Fisher
$6.95 pb * 210 pages * 0-910146-53-5

NOTES